CONTENTS

For Christa

MICHAEL ESSANY

GRMOLOGY

WHAT EVERY (SMART) GROOM NEEDS TO KNOW BEFORE THE WEDDING

Getting Involved, Helping Her Plan,
Respecting Tradition, Keeping Everyone Happy,
Handling the Big (and Small) Stuff,
and Everything that Really Matters Before You Walk Down the Aisle

SOURCEBOOKS CASABLANCA™
AN IMPRINT OF SOURCEBOOKS, INC.®
NAPERVILLE, ILLINOIS

Published by Sourcebooks Casablanca, an imprint of Sourcebooks, Inc.

P.O. Box 4410, Naperville, Illinois 60567-4410
(630) 961-3900
Fax: (630) 961-2168
www.sourcebooks.com

Library of Congress Cataloging-in-Publication Data

Essany, Michael.
 Groomology / Michael Essany.
    p. cm.
 Includes bibliographical references and index.
 1. Weddings--Planning. 2. Wedding etiquette. 3. Bridegrooms. I. Title.
 HQ745.E77 2009
 395.2'2--dc22

                            2008041427

           Printed and bound in the United States of America.
                          VP 10 9 8 7

ACKNOWLEDGMENTS

There is never a shortage of talented and inspiring people behind the genesis and execution of a worthwhile project. I owe this book in its entirety to a stable of truly outstanding and unfailingly supportive individuals.

The first, of course, is my beautiful wife Christa, whose love was the inspiration for my desire to become a better-than-average groom.

The concept for *Groomology*, a lighthearted study of the art of becoming an expert groom, arose from my own personal adventures. And if not for the foresight and commitment of Deb Werksman at Sourcebooks, this comprehensive lesson plan would have existed only for my benefit. Equally deserving of my appreciation and gratitude are Shana Drehs and Sara Kase, for their tireless efforts and invaluable input.

To my best friend since childhood, Mike Randazzo, who married his beautiful bride just one week before I married mine, thank you for being the perfect example of the kind of groom every bride deserves. Without your humor, support, and unfailing kindness, my existence today would have less substance than the plot of a David Hasselhoff movie.

Without the friendship, eternal support, and photographic talents of my good friend Ryan Musch of FH Photographic (www.fhphotographic.com) in Rensselaer, Indiana, my journey into the world of wedding planning would never have begun on such a positive note. Ryan and his beautiful family are an inspiration and a blessing to us all.

I certainly couldn't forget to thank my great friend Ian Ross Hughes, one of the most talented writers and funniest guys I have ever known. Your ideas, input, and humor have always been appreciated and serve only to improve everything about my own work. Thank you for letting a little bit of your greatness rub off on me.

Last but not least, I would like to thank and express my solidarity with a generation of grooms eager to tap into their groomologic potential and take an active role in helping plan their weddings, reducing the almost intolerable stress bearing down on their brides.

It is my fondest hope that this book will help you enjoy the journey, repel anxiety, and truly celebrate the relationship that led to this emotional roller coaster in the first place.

INTRODUCTION

I knew from across the room he was in serious trouble.

Fumbling with his coat and rummaging through his pockets, the cold glare from his fiancée told the whole story even before she spoke a word.

"How could you lose it?" she asked, with a whisper as loud as a shout.

"Relax," the groom reassured his bride while failing to conceal his own anxiety.

"It isn't enough that I have to do *everything* on that list," she said. "I guess I have to carry it now too."

"It's in the car," he quickly retorted, trying to convince himself as much as his bride.

Without further comment, the bride-to-be snatched the keys and headed for the parking lot. Naturally, those of us riveted by the unfolding drama had, for this man's sake, begun praying his brooding bride would find the elusive item in their vehicle.

Alas, however, their list was gone. And moments later, so was the bride. Upon realizing that her groom indeed had misplaced their sacred "to-do" list, she promptly bolted the premises and left her groom stranded at the local florist.

I offered the browbeaten man a ride home, but he calmly explained that he lived only a few miles down the road and wanted to "walk it off."

From time to time, I still wonder what became of that nameless groom who lost his list, his ride, and his bride on that crisp spring morning. I can't help but think of him whenever I spot other helpless—or, perhaps more fittingly, hapless—grooms thrown headfirst into the treacherous waters of wedding planning. But then it wasn't long ago that I had only to look in my own mirror to see such a pitiful example.

There are many things that can and usually do go wrong for first-time grooms. Since you're hopefully going to walk down the aisle only once in your life, you have to get it right the first time. You can't count on dress rehearsals to help you become the perfect groom someday. To be sure, being a dream groom is an uncommon feat, and frankly, one not commonly attempted. But, as it likely will turn out, both you and your fiancée will ultimately benefit from your willingness to boldly go where few men have gone before.

By now you probably have observed the many ways in which planning a wedding is among the most stressful and emotionally involving experiences of a woman's life. For the men who choose to go along on that journey, there's no end to the fascination of its mystifying twists and turns.

INSIDE THE MIND OF THE MARRYING FEMALE

Before we can address the new role of the contemporary groom, we must first understand the realities facing the contemporary bride, an extraordinary individual confronting even more extraordinary challenges.

For the typical marrying man, attempting to understand the full scope of his fiancée's emotions and the enormous expectations incumbent upon her could be the biggest mystery he will ever seek to unravel. But if many grooms struggle with understanding their bride-to-be's seemingly infinite burdens, the bride-to-be may also be engaged in an emotionally volatile process even she is struggling to understand.

Planning what hopefully will be the happiest day of her life can also be the most emotionally taxing and physically exhausting experience of her lifetime. The contemporary bride is bombarded with external pressures beyond anything yesterday's brides ever encountered.

You don't have to look beyond the corner newsstand or the latest reality television series to discover a myriad of examples of the ways weddings have become big business. Consequently, a leading cause of pre-wedding anxiety is the poor bride's attempts to meet the smorgasbord of unrealistic expectations that have been forced upon her by society, the media, and, of course, her closest friends and family.

In all but very few instances, the twenty-first-century bride can expect to contend with stresses created by:

- attempting to achieve the "perfect wedding"
- attempting to make every guest happy
- taking other people's criticisms personally
- trying to control factors that can't possibly be controlled
- stretching a budget and breaking the bank
- mediating family members who don't play well with others
- dealing with family and friends who want things done their own way
- forgetting to take personal downtime and failing to actually look forward to the wedding itself
- taking out frustrations on her fiancé

Unfortunately, not helping matters much is the average groom—a loving husband-to-be who regularly inspires the wrath of his beloved for not following cues, not completing tasks, or not being sensitive to his bride's needs.

Any modern groom under the (mis)impression that he's best off simply "staying out of her way" is undoubtedly putting himself in the path of extraordinary danger. Hell hath no fury like a bride neglected.

Time and time again, soon-to-be husbands only tackle the most obvious of tasks—the tangible duties and dilemmas (as detailed by the bride) that stand between the couple and the altar. But it is imperative to remember that what a bride directs her groom to do is only the beginning of a process. It's the unspoken responsibilities the contemporary groom takes on that can make all the difference in her world.

GROOMOLOGY

As you may have already deduced, groomology is the (sort of) scientific study of grooms who have been groomed for success.

Regrettably, the days of simply getting dressed and walking down the aisle have been relegated to an increasingly narrowing cultural subset. Today, men are encouraged to take a more proactive plunge. And as we'll learn, getting involved means more than merely asking the bride for a larger list of responsibilities.

It may be that the process under way is so intimidating to your beautiful bride that she gave you this book as an invitation to assume the uncommon role of a modern, savvy, involved groom—one who will ungrudgingly assist her in this enormous undertaking. Ready or not, guys, your future wives need what every marrying woman deserves but only a few receive—a smart, eternally supportive, hands-on groom.

I'm not merely trying to convince you to send spontaneous flowers or pamper your girl more than other grooms might (although that isn't a horrible idea). That's not your paramount aim, so you can put away your debit card. Being an *engaged* man does not refer simply to being engaged to be married. It also means being emotionally and physically engaged in the lengthy process of planning an event that, according to numerous published studies, is the source of more anxiety and emotional anguish than divorce or even death!

If you're like the majority of marrying men, you're almost certainly wondering why you should subject yourself to the tedious tasks emblazoned on your soon-to-be-wife's to-do list. Well, at the heart of groomology is the basic precept that being a contemporary groom is all about being your bride's hero, whether she admits to needing one or not. It's not about taking an equal role, or even a large role. Contrary to popular belief, it doesn't mean being a subservient minion to your authoritative bride. It doesn't mean your ideas and interests are unimportant, and it definitely doesn't suggest that you're a secondary player in a day that would be somewhat incomplete without you. It's about fashioning and playing a custom-made role that will benefit you as much as it does her.

Your mission, should you choose to accept it, is to reduce stress wherever possible, communicate effectively at every turn, and preemptively address the issues, concerns, and obstacles that routinely make wedding planning a nightmare for the girl you love and hope to spend the rest of your life with.

THE RULES OF GROOMOLOGY

1. Express legitimate interest in and concern for everything that matters to your bride.
2. Take over tasks your bride can't or won't do.
3. Be sensitive and responsive to your bride's needs and worries.
4. Be mindful of the relationship dynamics (who gets along and who doesn't) of all wedding participants and party planners.
5. Help your bride resolve both internal (emotional) as well as external conflicts.
6. Get her to relax by giving her a sweet surprise, a thoughtful card, or anything to remind her of why this headache is actually worth it.
7. Take time to learn all that is involved in planning and everything that is presently wracking her nerves.
8. Understand that every bride is different and expects different levels of involvement from her groom.
9. Be ready and able to give up your opinions if they are 1) proven wrong, 2) proven inappropriate, or 3) proven to upset your bride to a great extent.
10. Willingly accept the level of involvement your bride expects from you.
11. Be thoughtful and creative when it counts… and when it doesn't.
12. Be more patient with your bride than you have ever been before.

In addition to addressing the basic rules of this hands-on approach, *Groomology* will also help you begin conversations with your bride about who should do what, when, and why. In doing so, we preemptively address the elements of wedding planning that most frequently cause fights, diminish the groom, demonize the bride, divide families, and extinguish the romance of it all.

Chapter 1

GEARING UP

Gentlemen, the good old days are over.

As it turns out, our forefathers knew a premarital planning bliss that we will never personally experience. Never again will attending the wedding be the marrying man's most pressing responsibility. Today, the expected level of involvement continues to increase for modern grooms. And as we twenty-first-century grooms begin that trek down the contemporary aisle, it's important to recognize not only why this development is ultimately advantageous, but also how it came to be.

According to the U. S. Census, the median age for first-time marriages has risen sharply over the last four decades. As many wedding planners have begun documenting, when one's age increases, so too does one's level of interest and personal investment in the long process of wedding planning.

With more men and women marrying later in life, an obvious factor leading to an expanded role in planning for many grooms is maturity. In many instances, with age comes greater financial security, making it considerably less likely that a groom will want or need to hit up his parents—or his bride's parents—for money to bankroll the ceremony. Needless to say, if he's going to help foot the bill, he's certainly going to want to have a hand in managing his own money.

According to Carley Roney, editor-in-chief of theknot.com, it isn't uncommon to see a groom's role in the planning stages become more active once his money enters the picture. "Once your money's involved, you're going to care if its freesia or tulips," she says.

Such oversight leads to greater involvement, whether this is a conscious decision or not. In making arrangements and negotiating with vendors, grooms often become unexpectedly engrossed in the process. "They really want something that reflects them," says Roney.

Similarly, the modern bride is often a working woman, far more successful, educated, and self-sufficient than the brides of yesterday. As a result, the majority of today's betrothed females can't devote every waking moment to planning their wedding. Unfortunately, growing societal pressures and influences (analogous in many ways to high school peer pressure) add enormous stress to brides who feel the need to micromanage but don't have the time to execute the "perfect wedding" that society apparently dictates she must have—or else.

The underlying causes of modern grooms being more actively involved in wedding preparation are varied and complex. Yet, aside from the practical motives that inspire many a male to roll up their sleeves and book the caterer themselves, *why* a groom is involved is less significant than *how* he is involved.

THE ONE THING YOU NEED TO DO

Three years ago, an old college buddy informed me he was finally going to pop the question to his girlfriend of nearly six years. Soon after he bought the engagement ring, he went hog wild collecting every magazine, book, and DVD with the word "wedding" plastered on it. Hell-bent on being the best groom he could be, my good friend energetically overwhelmed himself—and his bride—with facts, figures, ideas, helpful suggestions, dos and don'ts, and creative tips. In no time at all, he was burned out, she was turned off, and although they were eventually happily married, the ceremony finally happened only after several delays and months of needless self-made stress.

I'll share a simple but imperative secret. Becoming an active planner in your own wedding doesn't begin where you might expect—reading bridal magazines, studying the art of wedding planning, or asking for a honey-do list. Becoming engaged in the planning process begins by engaging your fiancée in conversation.

THE BENEFIT OF VENTING

Forget the wedding magazines and bridal showcases. The first order of business for any groom looking to take the proactive plunge is to take his bride by the hand

and sincerely ask what her expectations are for the wedding. While she talks—and she probably will for quite a while—just listen. But listen intently, even if you don't really want to. Right now she needs to know that you care and that you truly want to be involved. Most important, however: the conversation you initiate will give her an invaluable opportunity to vent freely, something every bride occasionally needs for her own sanity.

Once you've opened the lines of communication, you may be surprised by what happens next. Either she will bombard you with ideas, suggestions, and outright directives, or she will simply express her appreciation for your interest and suggest only a minimal role for you in the coming months. At this point, though, it doesn't really matter how she foresees your role. In all likelihood, her needs and wants will noticeably transform as the planning stages progress.

Now you're probably thinking "Well, if she's going to change her mind so much anyway, why should I waste my time having a conversation with her about this stuff right now?" Fortunately, the real benefit to you from this bridal banter comes not from knowing what she specifically wants you to do. Instead, it comes from gaining insight into her expectations and apprehensions. Any valuable venting you can walk away with is the Holy Grail.

As we discussed earlier, the preeminent grooms of today aren't necessarily those who do the most mundane wedding planning chores. They are the ones who do the most to ease the stresses and burdens of their brides. There are many ways to do this, but unless you know exactly how your bride feels at the moment—regardless of how she may feel tomorrow—there is no possible way for you to plan for the challenges ahead.

Learning from your conversation (and a need may arise for more conversations) where her concerns lie and what her grand expectations are for the wedding, you will be able to take the steps necessary to help your bride relax and comfortably plan a magnificent wedding, and you will deservedly become an elite groom in your own right.

WHEN YOU SHOULD WALK AWAY

Not from the relationship, of course. And not from the wedding. But from the planning.

At some point in every man's life, he will be reminded by a woman—or by an incident with a woman—that it is absolutely vital to always think before speaking. Similarly, when breaching bridal territory and joining in on wedding planning, it is important to think before doing anything.

Once you've conferred with your fiancée about expectations and the obstacles in store, take a long walk all by your lonesome. If reflection isn't ordinarily your thing, try to muddle through at least this one time. Before you either follow the course charted by your partner or take it upon yourself to figure out what you should do, first clear your head and reflect on everything you know for certain about the wishes, fears, budget restrictions, et cetera that your fiancée has on her bustling mind. Concurrently, and just as critical to the process, consider all the uncertainties—all the aspects of wedding preparation that remain up in the air.

A few years ago, an engaged co-worker of mine took it upon himself to select—all on his own—his wedding invitations. As the story goes, my buddy found a "handsome" set of invitations (a box of fifty) in the clearance aisle of a local retailer. Although his fiancée didn't outright oppose the selection, a great deal of time was eventually wasted when their previously undetermined guest list wound up exceeding one hundred and no additional invitations of the same design were to be found anywhere. After squandering weeks looking for the same invitations, the couple finally abandoned the originals and started over with a new set that were available in an adequate quantity.

My co-worker friend was trying to be a proactive groom, but he started with an aspect of his wedding preparation that remained uncertain. What's the bottom line? If you're already positive that you and your fiancée want to spend your honeymoon someplace where it will be balmy and tropical, you can get busy booking the arrangements because you already have enough general information to make concrete plans that won't require a do-over. On the other hand, if the theme of your wedding is still undecided, don't bother bringing home the fluorescent Hawaiian centerpieces you found at K-mart.

Knowing what planning responsibilities can be helped and not hindered by your involvement is an advantage like no other. No matter how much time remains between now and your wedding, you should never approach any chore with a mind-set that there will be time to redo anything you don't get right the first time around. Know what's par for the course before taking your first swing.

Why Shopping for Candles Could Save the Day

After you make a thoughtful assessment of the process to come, begin to formulate an initial game plan. What should you do first?

Although it's imperative to gain as much insight as possible from wedding guides, books, and magazines, in the end, only so much of your preparation can come from printed resources. The time has finally come for you to venture out into the real world all by yourself.

Indeed, there's never been a more appropriate time to take a drive. Hit your local wedding boutiques, formal wear outfitters, retail outlets, novelty shops, and anyplace else you can find wedding stuff. You may be tempted to bring your fiancée, but you can't—at least not this time. Why? Because you need to keep distractions to a minimum when you're trying to study. And that's exactly what this expedition is about—studying.

You're not going to buy anything. You're not going to book anything. Chances are, you're not even going to touch anything. What you will do for certain, though, is learn a great deal about wedding products on the market.

All around the world, weddings are big business, not to mention being a magnet for suckers with a non-prioritized budget.

Take one box of unscented white tea lights, for example. In most places, you can get a set of one hundred for five bucks. But add the word "wedding" to the packaging of those same little candles, and watch the price balloon to ten bucks for a set of fifty.

A high priority on your fledgling to-do list should be taking a drive to four or five wedding-related stores in your neck of the woods, a task that should consume no more than a single morning or afternoon. Soak it all in. Take note of the options available. You probably had no idea that so many products and possibilities are out there. And even though you may initially find yourself bewitched, bothered, and bewildered by the sheer volume of crap you find dominating your window-shopping, the truth of the matter is that this private little rendezvous will make you a much savvier, informed groom.

The results of this field trip will prove far reaching. In no time at all, you'll find yourself in a better position to bounce creative ideas off your bride and even answer questions better than she may be able to. Best of all, you now can be trusted in her eyes to venture back into the wedding market to run errands now that she's aware that you're a bit wiser for the wear. Obviously, gaining her faith in your abilities to help plan the wedding is a significant step in reducing her overall stress.

WHEN DOING MORE IS LESS

By now, you're probably feeling quite the stud. You're informed, you're in touch, and you're seemingly in command of the challenges ahead.

Nonetheless, avoid the urge to fill your plate with things to do. You may be tempted to knock out all the planning in a flurry of activity, and then just relax the last six months before your wedding. A preferable alternative is to pace yourself throughout the planning stages. Don't forget, no matter how astute you may think you are now, both you and your bride will still botch something between now and the wedding; it may be trivial or it may be calamitous. By not getting too far ahead of yourself, you can assure that a minor disaster doesn't become a major one or have a domino effect on other elements of your plans you rushed through just to convince yourself you're somehow ahead of the game.

In every phase of the process unfolding before you, take small steps. Even for the involved groom, no matter how you cut it, the bride is still going to have more work and stress than you can ever imagine. Don't overload yourself to the point where you become unavailable to do your most important job—help the bride when she gets overloaded.

WEDDINGS ARE A TEAM SPORT

For whatever reason, many men believe it is contrary to the nature of a smart, self-sufficient groom to have to double check with his bride if it's "all right" to do something. Whether it's surprising the bride by booking wedding flowers all by yourself or selecting the men's attire without any discussion, such gung-ho behavior has a huge potential for backfiring.

Even if you're taking charge in the planning process, it's absolutely imperative that you take nothing for granted. It may seem counterproductive to call your bride on her cell phone to check with her each time you make a purchase or spur-of-the-moment decision you assume she will agree with. Put that notion out of your head immediately. The potential reward of taking something for granted and getting it right is not worth the risk of getting it wrong.

When it comes down to making important decisions on the spot, even ones placed squarely in your court, don't assume anything. Doing things on your own is in no way the same as doing things about which she is unaware. Being entrenched in the planning of your wedding does not give you bridal immunity. It is always a good idea to check in with your fiancée to ensure you're both on the same page about product selection, service bookings, or any other arrangement, small or substantial. Believe me, she won't be annoyed with a call to check that whatever you're about to decide is desirable to her and appropriate for your wedding. In fact, she will probably appreciate it tremendously.

IT'S YOUR WEDDING, TOO

This is a sensitive, delicate issue, but one that deserves acknowledgment.

I have yet to meet an involved groom who has not, at some point during the labored wedding planning process, developed his own vision for the wedding and consequently butted heads with his bride over some aspect of the ceremony, reception, or honeymoon.

So far, much of this book has been devoted to deferring to your bride's wishes, wants, and worries. Even so, it is only fair that in the grand scheme of things, you should not be expected to silence your heartfelt opinions if they grossly conflict with those of your fiancée.

As you likely have experienced by now, there's no such thing as a wedding that is planned from start to finish without the bride and groom having at least one knock-down, drag-out disagreement about some element of the big day. In the past, a majority of arguments sprang from men meddling with who should or shouldn't be invited. Today, however, with men being more financially and emotionally invested in their weddings, it is far more common for grooms to have a strong opinion about other aspects of the wedding—the theme, menu, music, et cetera.

This is your day, too. And you deserve to be represented. As a result, you have every right to take a stand when you feel strongly about any concern pertinent to your wedding. And in most cases, you can peacefully negotiate—if the stand you take is articulated in a manner every bit as sweet and thoughtful as your involvement has been thus far.

Never demand that your ideas be accepted because "I'm paying for it" or because "I'm doing a lot of work." Appeal to her with the sincere passion of your wishes. Most arguments during wedding planning happen because one party demands to have his or her own way. Keep demands to a minimum.

Ultimately, however, remember that the wedding means an awful lot less than your marriage will. I'm guessing that by your golden anniversary, neither of you will remember what you argued about before the wedding or who ultimately got their way.

Put every disagreement in perspective, and make the deals you need to make to get things rolling smoothly. Ironically, sometimes not getting your way can work more to your advantage than the other way around. Call it a hunch or a bizarre fact of nature, but the world seems to be a much happier and more hospitable place for grooms when their brides are happy.

LEAVE YOUR COMFORT ZONE

In the months preceding my wedding, I often felt intimidated by the enormity of the process unfolding around me. On occasion, I couldn't help but shy away from some planning responsibilities, because I felt so utterly out of sorts.

Over time, however, I grew to learn the value of taking

chances. While I never took it upon myself to select funky altar flowers or decide on a bizarre menu without my fiancée's input, I did eventually grow more comfortable in my new role as supergroom.

When a specific planning responsibility was put under my command, I dealt with it as best I could. But sometimes, when out and about on my own, I also would formulate off-the-wall ideas for our wedding (party favors, wedding themes, etc.). Most of the time, such ideas would make my fiancée laugh at the shear absurdity of whatever I was proposing. But my willingness to embrace aspects of wedding planning that were altogether foreign to my skill set eventually did prove fruitful—albeit accidentally on occasion.

During the weeks and months before our wedding, I attended more than a few bridal shows and vendor expos within a hundred mile radius. At one of the shows I visited, I found a company that made wedding tiaras exactly to the liking of my fiancée. Christa entered a drawing to win a free tiara and, incredibly, she won. Even though I thought the free Miller Light T-shirt I won as a door prize was cooler, my willingness to venture out into territory unfamiliar for grooms produced positive results—for me *and* my fiancée.

Now and then, even an amateur's eye can spot a needle in a haystack. Taking a chance and bouncing your own wacky ideas off your bride can be good for a laugh, spark an original idea in another facet of wedding planning, or legitimately serve to improve the look or execution of your ceremony or reception.

Creativity in a groom—that is, creativity that is discussed before it is applied—never harmed any wedding. Do you know not a thing about wedding centerpieces? Try to come up with a creative idea for one and share it with your bride anyway. Of course, don't be devastated when she tells you your idea is dreadful. Instead, learn from the "error" and continue applying your ingenuity elsewhere when the situation allows.

Several weeks before our wedding, I suggested to my fiancée that we deck the reception hall with loads of personal relationship memorabilia. Being sentimental pack rats, we both had amassed impressive collections of romantic notes, poems, drawings, receipts from memorable dates, et cetera. Although Christa didn't care for the idea of tattered love notes adorning our elegant reception site, she was inspired by the idea. Her solution was to decorate the banquet hall with something unique and relevant to our wedding, but far removed from the sappy and sloppy artifacts of our courtship.

Because she'd worked as a kindergarten aide the year before our wedding, the kids from school (and their parents, of course) threw a bridal shower for Christa in which each child drew or made a wedding card for us. The inventory of their creative works was so adorable— not to mention plentiful—that we were able to decorate a small wing of our reception hall with these charming works of art.

So even though my initial idea was shot down, the thought inspired a light bulb to go off over Christa's head that resulted in a beautiful finishing touch for our reception site's decor.

TAKE TIME FOR YOURSELF TOO

A vital aspect of groomology is understanding how and when to shield your fiancée from the stress factors that bombard the typical bride. There's nothing more unpleasant and distracting from the joys of a wedding than being frazzled and burned out right before—or on—your wedding day.

But what's true for the bride is also true for the groom. Any groom actively engaged in wedding preparation is bound to absorb or share the frustrations common to the average bride. As a result, it is key for a proactive groom to not let his own stress rub off on the bride—this obviously would be counterproductive to this entire endeavor.

Throughout the process, take time to step back from the business of wedding planning. But don't take a break and leave your bride in the dust. Facilitate a date night or weekend getaway for you both to enjoy one another and forget about the anxiety-ridden planning process. Remember, the wedding is merely a conduit for a loving marriage to follow.

In chapter six, "The Other To-Do List," we'll discuss a wide array of romantic gestures and stress-relieving tactics that can ease your bride's worries and stresses. Let such activities do the same for you.

KEEP YOUR EYE ON THE PRIZE

Throughout the months of planning to come, never take your eye off the joyful end result of all your hard work. The bows you can then take will be well deserved and will signal the grand finale of a process you ultimately will be glad you embarked upon.

GETTING IN THE MOOD

One of the most fun and relaxing ways to prepare for a wedding (not to mention pick up a few good ideas from fictionalized grooms) is to check out some of the many romantic flicks from the massive inventory of wedding-related blockbusters that have been making audiences laugh, cry, and think for decades.

Here are a few personal favorites that may also get you in the mood.

1. **Wedding Crashers (2005)** - *Starring Owen Wilson & Vince Vaughn*
2. **Everyone Says I Love You (1996)** *Starring Drew Barrymore & Edward Norton*
3. **Moonstruck (1987)** - *Starring Cher & Nicolas Cage*
4. **The Princess Bride (1987)** - *Starring Cary Elwes & Robin Wright Penn*
5. **Meet the Parents (2000)** - *Starring Ben Stiller & Robert De Niro*
6. **Only You (1994)** - *Starring Marisa Tomei & Robert Downey Jr.*

7. **Sabrina (1954)** - *Starring Humphrey Bogart & Audrey Hepburn (Please, the original only!)*

8. **Father of the Bride (1991)** - *Starring Steve Martin & Kimberly Williams*

9. **The Wedding Singer (1998)** - *Starring Adam Sandler & Drew Barrymore*

10. **My Big Fat Greek Wedding (2002)** - *Starring Nia Vardalos & John Corbett*

CHAPTER 2

THE PRENUPTIAL
LANDSCAPE

Congratulations! You are about to embark on an extraordinary endeavor few men ever consider—at least not without substantial encouragement or a few beers.

Your challenge is to gain a bird's-eye view of the tightly wound, schedule-focused brain of your bride—that vast mysterious wonderland that, for all its emotional upheavals, remains anchored by the almighty wedding to-do list and its deadlines. Understanding the calendar-crazy focus of your fiancée's frontal lobe is your first step in coming to understand your bride-to-be's thoughts, fears, and overall mind-set.

Taking a good look at what's ahead from her unique (and overwhelmed) perspective, it's easy to see how the underpinnings of stress begin so early. Planning a wedding can be an unimaginably awesome task for a bride, so it's important to take a look at the planning stages that lie ahead for the coming weeks and months. *The first step to becoming a successful groom is becoming an informed groom.*

NUPTIALS BY THE NUMBERS

- *In the United States, 2.3 million couples marry each year. That's 6,200 weddings a day!*
- *The median number of wedding guests is 178.*
- *The typical bride in the United States is 25.3 years of age. The typical groom is 26.9.*
- *Nearly one-third of individuals tying the knot have previously walked down the aisle.*

Source: U.S. Census

The following is a bare-bones wedding calendar that will be delved into in greater detail throughout the book. This twelve-month delineation of duties and deadlines is a preliminary glimpse at all that your fiancée is facing.

Every bride is exceptional in terms of her own distinct style, preferences, and nature of concerns. Nonetheless, the stress scale I've applied, which ranges from one to five, illustrates the looming responsibilities that frequently cause the most anxiety for the average bride. Naturally, not everyone can or should follow such a specific time line. It's merely a general template that may be molded to suit your unique situation.

12 Months Before the Wedding

Select a wedding date.

Without question, this is one of your biggest decisions, and it should never be taken lightly. Although superb weddings have been pulled off in less time, it is prudent to allow at least a twelve-month time line for planning. When selecting a date, however, be certain to thoughtfully consider your general hopes and ambitions for the wedding. If, for instance, your bride is dreaming of a winter wonderland theme, don't schedule a spring wedding. Also, take time to consult family and friends with regard to scheduling. The last thing you need is to learn that your wedding date is inconvenient for half the people you plan to invite. Overall, as long as your date suits your wishes, it should be safe to proceed without lingering concerns.

Get organized.

Whether you use a shoe box or a filing cabinet, organizing your most important wedding-related papers is key and will likely begin with storing your contract for the reception hall or banquet facility. If your bride is an organized gal, you're in luck. If not, get on the ball! Without strong organization, the planning process can quickly turn her dream wedding into an absolute nightmare.

Set the budget.

Unless you're a member of Congress, there's an excellent possibility that you comprehend the basic logic of not spending more money than you currently have. Carefully consider your situation, then determine a budget before any bills are incurred.

ASKING PERMISSION

For some grooms, the notion of asking the bride's father for permission to marry his daughter is downright silly and somewhat embarrassing. Yet for many brides and their families, it may be desirable or even mandatory. The issue may be pointless to broach if you and your bride have already determined the proper course of action in your unique situation. However, a great majority of premarital clashes are born of matters exactly like this one.

If you're this far along with planning your wedding and you still haven't asked for permission, it's a safe bet that you're not planning to. Of course, that was exactly my line of thinking until our rehearsal dinner, when I finally asked my future father-in-law (less than twenty-four hours before the wedding) if I could take his daughter's hand in marriage. Pleased that I finally asked, we chuckled about the whole process before he kindly bestowed his blessing upon our impending nuptials.

Despite seeming sexist and old-fashioned, the tradition of requesting permission remains popular because so many brides—and their fathers—maintain it's the polite thing to do. The good news is, if your bride is adamant about you seeking permission, there's a good chance she already knows the answer you'll get.

For some men, it is just "beneath them" to request permission from the first man his fiancée ever loved. That may be a natural feeling, but it's not a legitimate excuse to get out of going through with it, and if your fiancée and her family feel it is important, there is no reason not to humor them. Understandably, this is difficult for some grooms to accept. But the alternative—starting a new life on the wrong foot with your bride's family— is even less desirable. Take the five minutes and ask permission for what you already know will be granted.

Determine the rough size of the guest list.

Is it going to be a big wedding or a small wedding? Big wedding, small reception? Small wedding, big reception? Do you want a lot of guests, or only the ones most important to you? Planning can't begin in earnest until you answer these vital questions.

Choose the style and theme.

Before you can entertain the particulars of your wedding, you must determine if your event will be formal, semiformal, or informal, and whether there will be a theme. Although your bride will have her own preferences, so will everyone else. As groom, your role will be to remind your bride that nobody's opinion matters more than hers.

Capture your glory.

Notify the local papers of your engagement. Even if you don't care about all the excitement and attention, make the announcement for the sake of posterity and keep it in your soon-to-follow wedding album.

Pick the key players.

Before asking anyone to be in your bridal party, create a list of possibilities and backups. Take a few weeks to give some thought to this. You'll be glad you did later.

Consider a consultant.

If you're thinking of hiring a wedding consultant, don't bring an expert aboard midstream. Explore your options (and the corresponding expenses) early, and then decide if a consultant is warranted, unnecessary, or even financially possible.

Choose your venues.

The selection of the ceremony site and reception venue is often delayed until it's too late to secure your first choice. The selection of a venue can clearly illustrate the law of supply and demand—there is a limited supply of "perfect venues" and a great demand for those that exist, especially within a budget. For this reason, it's vital to reserve your preferred location for your scheduled wedding date as soon as possible.

Purchase a wedding gown. 🐚🐚🐚🐚

One of the most exciting but stressful elements of wedding planning for any bride is selecting her wedding gown, a process that could take upward of a year to complete. You're bound to hear a healthy intermingling of glee and gloom about this process from the time the gown is purchased until the moment it finally accompanies her down the aisle. Although conventional wisdom has it that there is little for the groom to do while the bride is busy browsing, nothing could be farther from the truth. In reality, the stress levels experienced by a bride in search of her gown can be astounding. There may never be a more opportune occasion to pamper and calm your bride, by whatever means necessary.

MARRIAGE BY THE MONEY

- *Modern couples bankroll their own weddings almost 30 percent of the time. The bride's family foots the bill 17 percent of the time. But more than half of all contemporary weddings are now financed through intermingled funds from family, friends, and, of course, the happy couple.*
- *The typical wedding budget is approximately $20,000.*
- *The average honeymoon budget is $3,600.*
- *More than 90 percent of couples register for gifts. They receive gifts from an average of two hundred guests.*
- *The average wedding guest spends anywhere from $70 to $100 on a wedding gift.*

source: www.Brides.com

10 Months Before the Wedding

Choose your professionals.

There is no shortage of experts needed for even the simplest of ceremonies and receptions. From the DJ, caterer, and photographer to the wedding planner, there are countless professionals to hire and only a limited budget available. You'll need to decide how many professionals you can pay for; interview several, and hire the best you can afford.

Finalize your bridal party.

By now you've had a few months to ponder and have promoted your closest family and friends into the elite class that is your bridal party. Notify your nominees and make sure they are willing, available, and can commit to participating before they are fitted for wedding attire.

Choose the wedding officiant.

Whether it's a person of the cloth or a person of the law, waiting until the last minute to select a wedding officiant is a common mistake. Like any other vendor, individuals qualified to officiate a wedding ceremony are professionals with busy schedules. If you and your bride already know whom you would like to officiate the service, make an effort to secure his or her services before another couple does. (In some states, you can even have a friend or family member deputized as a justice of the peace, and they can perform the ceremony.)

Select your attire.

The style and color of both the bridesmaid's dresses and men's attire should be determined with ample time to spare. Although this process seems incredibly straightforward and rooted in personal preferences, it is commonly one of the greatest sources of stress for the bride. Why? Because whether you realize it or not, there is a difference between cream and eggshell. Finding the right look through the skillful coordination of colors, accessories, and patterns is likely to be important to your bride. For this reason, it also should be important to you. Help her sift through the options, and provide your honest feedback. After all, you'll be wearing this stuff too.

Compile the guest list.

Yet another important but equally nerve-racking chore is narrowing down your list of potential wedding guests. You've already estimated the desired size of your wedding, and, chances are, you probably compiled a list of virtually everyone you know. At this point, however, it's time to do some deleting to get it down to a preferred list of guests. Just be sure not to forget to provide your families with an opportunity to invite their own guests, within an agreed-upon limit, of course. This will help reduce the prospect of added stress over who should or shouldn't be invited.

CEREMONIES BY THE SEASON

According to the Greeting Card Association (www.greetingcard.org) the most popular months for weddings are:

1. June
2. August
3. May
4. July
5. September
6. October

7. December
8. November
9. April
10. February
11. March
12. January

8 MONTHS BEFORE THE WEDDING

Confirm the guest list.

One of the toughest decisions you'll have to make must be made at least eight months prior to the wedding. Since most invited guests ultimately attend, it's important only to invite those on your preferred list—that is, the narrowed list of potential guests you created a couple months ago. Although many couples are tempted to pad the number to account for those who don't RSVP, don't do so. There's an excellent possibility that some guests will attend without having had the courtesy to first RSVP.

Select wedding invitations.

With the guest list finalized, invitations may be ordered. For convenience and consistency, wedding invitations and thank-you cards should be designed and purchased together.

Select save the date postcards or magnets 🐚

After selecting your wedding invitations, you may choose to make or order "save the date" magnets or postcards, which typically precede the actual invitations and are usually mailed anywhere from four to six months prior to the wedding.

Establish a gift registry. 🐚

Unless you have a need for three toasters and seven coffeemakers, a gift registry is the only practical way to politely direct would-be gift-givers toward your preferred wedding presents. It's best to be mindful, of course, of aiming the registry gun at both high- and low-end products to accommodate the diverse budgets of your wedding guests.

DEBATING A DESTINATION?

To those for whom money is no object, Forbes *magazine's list of the most luxurious honeymoon destinations may provide a helpful guide.*

From the lush and secluded Grand Mercury Island in New Zealand to The Palazzo Vendramin, a 15th-century residence in part of the Grand Hotel Cipriani in Venice, Italy, there are plenty of lavish locations for a well-financed honeymoon.

Of course, we're not all high-rolling honeymooners. Yet there are scores of high caliber and surprisingly affordable destination wedding locales. As any reputable travel agent will attest, there is no scarcity of hot deals at group rates. From a sunny beach romp in south Florida to a fly fishing trip in northern Alaska, destination weddings may not be as expensive you would expect. So even if you're on a tight budget, you may be able to afford a destination wedding more elegant than a drive-though service led by an Elvis impersonator in Vegas.

Just be sure to bear in mind the general rules that accompany a destination wedding:

- *The happy couple provides all hotel accommodations at the resort, including food and drinks for their guests.*
- *The wedding guests pay for airfare and any other ancillary expenses.*
- *The destination wedding is typically a three-day weekend for guests while it generally continues a full week for the bride and groom.*

Source: *Forbes*

6 MONTHS BEFORE THE WEDDING

Spring for the bands.

No, we're not talking about the music yet. Selecting wedding bands, a joint venture for most couples, can be tricky. The six-month mark is a good time to begin browsing and pricing. If all goes as planned, these rings will be with you as long as your partner is. Give the process sufficient effort to ensure you will be happy with the wedding bands you choose for as long as you both shall live.

Explore honeymoon destinations.

Although the Internet has made it surprisingly easy to research potential honeymoon locations, the ultimate decision depends upon budget restrictions and personal preference. Generally speaking, in order to secure the best rates (and to expedite removal of this looming responsibility from the to-do list), the sooner the honeymoon is booked (usually by the groom) the better off you'll be.

Talk dinner.

If your banquet hall doesn't include a dining package, you will have to find an outside caterer to provide the wedding dinner. Six months prior to the wedding is an excellent time to begin discussing menu options and potential caterers.

Choose a wedding cake.

This ornate dessert that gets shoved into the bride and groom's faces will certainly be more slowly enjoyed and savored by the many guests in attendance. When selecting a wedding cake, thoughtfully consider flavor and size to please and accommodate as many guests as possible. In the years ahead, guests may not remember much about your wedding, but they will remember the cake if it's as delicious and plentiful as it is glamorous.

Recommend travel and lodging accommodations.

Since it's quite probable that at least one out-of-town guest will attend your wedding, it is polite and practical to begin looking into travel and overnight accommodations for guests as early as possible. Although it isn't necessarily a bride or groom's responsibility to actually make travel arrangements, it may be helpful to prepare a list of recommendations or even reserve blocks of overnight accommodations at select local hotels that often offer the advantage of group discounts.

WEDDING BUDGET BREAKDOWN

Here is a rough breakdown of typical wedding expenses. These numbers are derived from an average of multiple wedding budgets and what percentage was allocated for each aspect.

Food — 12%	*Invitations — 3%*
Reception and Rentals — 10%	*Gifts and Favors — 4%*
Attire — 12%	*Wedding Rings — 2%*
Flowers — 8%	*Ceremony — 2%*
Photography — 5%	*Transportation — 1%*
Videography — 2%	*Miscellaneous — 4%*
Music — 7%	*Tips and taxes — 5%*

Source: *Better Homes & Gardens*

4 MONTHS BEFORE THE WEDDING

Order or make the wedding party favors.

Making or purchasing wedding party favors may seem an incredibly basic task, but it can be one of the most time-consuming and stressful of chores. Of course, that doesn't mean that making party favors can't be fun. In fact, many couples allow the task's potential tediousness to overshadow the invaluable opportunity for the quality time together that a massive arts and crafts project of this nature can provide. Just being with her, lending a hand, and maybe inspiring a few laughs is more than sufficient to transform this chore into a memorable pleasure.

Book the florist.

Weddings and flowers go hand in hand. The selection of flowers and a preferred florist is a major decision that, while certainly not the most stressful task, still requires enormous reserves of time and energy.

Begin the legal circus.

From changing her name (and the name on her bills, student loans, driver's license, etc.) to establishing a joint bank account and changing the beneficiaries of life insurance policies, getting married involves a lot of legal changes. The research regarding these and other legal processes should begin well before vows are exchanged.

Provide or prepare to give deposits.

At least ninety days prior to the wedding, a number of service providers may begin to invoice or request deposits. This is an ideal time to review services to be rendered and finalize details.

Book the honeymoon.

One could ponder honeymoon destinations endlessly. But by the four-month mark, couples should confirm their plans, book all travel and accommodations, and obtain any needed visas or other travel-related documents.

3 Months Before the Wedding

Schedule the rehearsal dinner.

A wedding rehearsal is vitally important to the big day going smoothly. And whether it's a formal affair at a banquet hall or a relaxed barbeque at a family member's home, the rehearsal dinner is a welcome added perk of the occasion. Not only does the rehearsal dinner provide a much needed opportunity to gather, relax, spend quality time, and share a meal together, it also extends a celebration that, when all is said and done, will seem to have gone by much too fast.

Begin tuxedo fittings.

Assemble the groomsmen at your chosen tuxedo rental business and let the measurements fly.

Book related transportation services.

If a limo is in order for the ceremony or reception, make appropriate arrangements while an inventory of luxury vehicles is still available for your wedding date.

Rent all necessary items.

There's a strong possibility that your wedding will require the rental of various items (centerpieces, crystal, chocolate fountains, etc.). Unless you have a wedding planner who is handling such reservations, it's important to arrange to rent what you need at least three months before the wedding.

Schedule relevant consultations.

Meeting with your wedding officiant can be helpful, enjoyable, and surprisingly relaxing. It's also an opportunity to gain insight into other responsibilities still to be tackled or expectations that may need to be revised.

Purchase bridal party gifts.

An often overlooked item on the to-do list is finding a small gift for each member of the bridal party. It's a courteous gesture that can easily slip through the cracks if delayed until the hectic few weeks leading up to the wedding.

ENGAGING STATISTICS

- *The winter holidays remain the most popular time of year to get engaged, particularly December, which has as many engagements (15%) as November and January combined (each 6%).*

- *In the United States, the typical engagement period spans fourteen months.*

- *The average altar-bound woman is now 27 years old and her husband-to-be is 29.*

Source: Conde Nast Bridal Group

---

2 MONTHS BEFORE THE WEDDING

Mail the invitations.

If there is a quintessential moment when you finally realize this wedding is really going to happen, it's when you mail the perfectly prepared wedding invitations that probably have been dwelling in your desk for several weeks, if not months. No fewer than eight weeks prior to the ceremony, put the formal invites in the snail mail and then patiently await the RSVPs.

Schedule formal-wear fittings and alterations.

Final fittings for the wedding gown, bridesmaid dresses, and tuxedos should be scheduled with ample time before the wedding to spare in the likely event that further changes will be warranted.

Select wedding music.

Whether you have a band or DJ, it's important to be hands-on in selecting specific songs for the reception, particularly the first dance. Provide your hired maestro with your preferences long before the wedding in case he or she does not have ready access to the music requested.

Prepare the wedding vows.

If you and your fiancée are preparing your own vows, there obviously will be more to do than just repeat the words of your presiding minister. There are a few general rules to follow in preparing vows. First, agree with your fiancée upon a length for each of your vows. The last thing you want is for her to prepare three pages of glowing content and you respond with three short sentences. Second, although each of you should spend time alone reflecting on what you'd like to say, decide whether you are going to write your vows together or separately. Third, use lots of expressive words and phrases to adequately communicate your thoughts and emotions. Make certain to be as descriptive as possible. If, for example, your beautiful bride makes you laugh a lot, take note of what she does or how she does it. (It might help to use Web resources or self-help guides to review other people's vows and study how they were prepared.) Fourth, ask your fiancée, minister, or close friends or family members to review what you've written and offer input to help polish it. Fifth, don't be afraid to use humor or tell a brief lighthearted story that captures what your bride means to you. Finally, practice, practice, practice! Naturally, it isn't uncommon for a groom to get a little choked up or nervous during the formal reading of vows at the wedding ceremony. However, the better you know them (and are used to their emotional wallop), the better off and more comfortable you will be.

Check with the florist.

Make certain that orders were properly placed and reconfirm any delivery details.

Design the ceremony or service programs.

Unless a wedding planner has accepted this responsibility, this is the appropriate time to begin customizing your wedding programs. Whether you're having them professionally made or printing them yourself at home, the same general information will need to be contained within the finished product. Think of your wedding program as a theater playbill—the who, what, when, where, and why of the occasion should all be laid out. In other words, your program should include: Information about/order of the service; the names of the wedding party members; the hymn(s), if there will be music; the names of the bride and groom's parents; a personal thank-you message from you and your bride; and any additional pertinent information relating to either the ceremony or the reception to follow (e.g., the time, location, and directions to the reception site).

Select your wedding accessories.

Whether it's something new or something borrowed, there are some things that take a while to get just right. Selecting wedding accessories (which may include everything from shoes for her to cuff links for you) remains an exciting but occasionally frustrating process.

1 MONTH BEFORE THE WEDDING

The final countdown begins.

Although the last month of wedding planning is much too detailed, intensive, and—let's face it—frightening to consider in depth in this second chapter, it's important to understand that the planning process is like running a marathon. The race begins slowly, picks up a consistent pace, and then turns unbelievably grueling for the last couple of miles. And although the groom has typically been allowed to pace himself for the whole duration, the bride is usually running at full speed from the start.

Fortunately for your fiancée, this deceptively straight-forward calendar is replete with opportunities for you to be her greatest cheerleader and helpmate. But before we can begin the discussion of your role as a modern groom, it's important to understand traditional wedding–related responsibilities and to whom they are traditionally delegated, something we will cover in the next chapter.

NOT YOUR EVERYDAY NUPTIALS

The night before our rehearsal dinner, my fiancée and I found a rare moment of tranquility amidst the frenetic atmosphere to which we had grown accustomed. Wanting to tune out our apprehensions, we tuned in for some brainless entertainment on cable. Appropriately, that evening VH1 broadcast a special program showcasing the twenty most expensive celebrity weddings of all time.

As we sat there watching the story of pop idol Madonna's wedding with film director Guy Ritchie in December 2000 at Scotland's Skibo Castle, we were awed by the footage of a wedding that cost per person what our wedding would cost in total. Our fascination continued as we watched Sting, Gwyneth Paltrow, and Rupert Everett arrive at the castle, where Madonna famously donned a 1910 diamond tiara once worn by Princess Grace of Monaco.

Indeed, these aren't your everyday nuptials. Yet, for some reason, an ungodly number of couples preparing for the plunge allow these lavish merrymakings to cloud their thoughts and diminish the excitement about their much more modest ceremonies.

Looking back, Christa and I didn't have a wedding nearly as elaborate, expensive, or tabloid worthy as Madonna and Guy Ritchie's wedding. But, at least we're still married.

My point? Don't get caught up in the nauseating nuptials of celebrities. Anyone who tells you that a wedding must be lavish, ornate, and completely removed from "everyday nuptials" is completely missing the point.

The overabundance of attention given Hollywood marriages by the perennially nosy mainstream media has seriously impaired the average bride and groom's ability to separate the wedding from the marriage. At the end of the day, a wedding is merely a flashy informality; a legal conduit to a lifetime of happiness that, hopefully, will bestow memories richer than any movie star in the world.

Chapter 3

Respecting and Revising Tradition

Traditionally, members of the bridal party, along with other key players in the planning stages, have significant yet very different responsibilities. The collective goal of these individuals is to ease the enormous pressures weighing on the bride and groom before, during, and after the ceremony.

But do you want to know a dirty little secret about the process to come? Some members of the bridal party always manage to create stress rather than reduce it—particularly for the bride. So it is absolutely essential for any groom looking to support his bride through the challenging stages ahead to first understand the traditional roles played by the bridal party and the responsibilities entrusted to specific members.

The following summary of duty distribution is not even remotely set in stone. But for her sake, it may be easier to first understand tradition before trying to revise it.

The Bride

- Selects wedding gown, accessories, and hairstyle.
- Consults with groom and family about the wedding budget.
- Determines the location of the ceremony and reception.
- Prepares her vows.
- Hires a wedding planner, photographer, DJ or band, caterer, and other professionals as needed.
- Chooses her maid of honor and bridesmaids.
- Selects bridesmaid dresses.
- Chooses music for the reception.
- Selects a florist and wedding flowers.
- Designs or selects wedding invitations.
- Compiles names for guest list with help from the groom.
- Addresses and mails wedding invitations.
- Purchases the groom's wedding ring.
- Obtains and organizes all necessary paperwork for name change, insurance, bank accounts, and any travel-related documents for the honeymoon if necessary (passports, birth certificates, etc.).
- Makes or purchases a wedding gift for the groom.
- Makes or purchases wedding gifts for her bridesmaids.

TRADITIONAL EXPENSES FOR THE BRIDE

- *Invitations and thank-you notes*
- *Wedding presents for bridesmaids*
- *Accommodations and lodging for bridesmaids*
- *Wedding programs*
- *The Guest Book*

THE GROOM

- Purchases the bride's engagement and wedding rings.
- Prepares his vows.
- Helps the bride compile the guest list.
- Chooses a best man and other groomsmen.
- Selects his tuxedo and formal wear for the groomsmen.
- Makes or purchases wedding gifts for his groomsmen.
- Arranges limo service or other transportation for the wedding day.
- Applies for and obtains a marriage license (and brings it to the ceremony).
- Books and pays for the honeymoon.
- Obtains any required travel-related documents for the honeymoon.
- Pays for the bridal bouquet and all floral accessories for the wedding party.
- Purchases a card and wedding gift for bride.
- Assists in additional ceremony and reception planning as directed by the bride.

TRADITIONAL EXPENSES FOR THE GROOM

- *The bride's engagement and wedding rings*
- *Marriage license*
- *Religious leader or wedding officiant's fee*
- *Rental or purchase of his formal wear*
- *Gifts for the groomsmen*
- *The bride's bouquet*
- *Boutonnieres for groomsmen and flowers for both mothers and grandmothers*
- *Honeymoon*

THE MAID (OR MATRON) OF HONOR

- Helps the bride select the wedding gown.
- Assists in the selection of bridesmaid dresses.
- Purchases her own dress and accompanying accessories.
- Helps the bride choose the wedding flowers.
- Plans the bridal shower and bachelorette party.
- Takes note of all presents given to the couple at the bridal shower.
- Prepares and delivers a brief speech for the reception.
- Assists in the decoration of the ceremony location and reception hall.
- Participates in the wedding rehearsal and attends the rehearsal dinner.

- Helps to coordinate the responsibilities of the bridesmaids.
- Holds onto the groom's ring until the ceremony begins.
- Tends to the bride's veil and train before and during the ceremony.
- Dances at the reception with the best man.
- Serves as a gracious hostess at the reception.

TRADITIONAL EXPENSES FOR THE MAID (OR MATRON) OF HONOR

- *Bridal shower*
- *Her maid of honor dress and shoes*
- *Hair and make up for the wedding*
- *Bachelorette party*

THE BRIDESMAIDS

- Purchase their dresses and accessories for the wedding.
- Assist in the planning of the bridal shower and/or bachelorette party.
- Help decorate the reception hall and prepare wedding favors.
- Run errands as needed by the bride.
- Attend rehearsal and rehearsal dinner.

- Help the bride before and during the wedding as directed.
- Serve as gracious hostesses during the reception.

TRADITIONAL EXPENSES FOR THE BRIDESMAIDS

- *Bridesmaid dress and shoes*
- *Personal travel expenses*
- *Contributions to bridal shower and/or bachelorette party*

THE BEST MAN

- Rents or purchases his wedding formal wear.
- Throws the bachelor party for the groom.
- Participates in the wedding rehearsal.
- Provides transportation to the ceremony for the groom.
- Handles compensation of clergy/officiant.
- Talks to the groom and eases his nerves before the ceremony.
- Provides transportation for the newlyweds to the reception.
- Ensures that groomsmen and ushers are organized and informed.
- Holds onto the bride's wedding ring until the ceremony begins.

- Accompanies maid (or matron) of honor down the aisle.
- Escorts the maid (matron) of honor during the recessional.
- Prepares and delivers a brief speech for the reception.
- Stands in the receiving line.
- Dances with the maid (or matron) of honor and encourages others to dance.
- Provides transportation of the newlyweds to their hotel suite.
- Returns the rented wedding formal wear for all the men in the bridal party.

TRADITIONAL EXPENSES
FOR THE BEST MAN

- *Personal wedding formal wear*
- *Bachelor party*
- *Personal travel expenses*
- *Personal hotel accommodations*

GROOMSMEN AND USHERS

- Purchase or rent their own wedding attire.
- Schedule and keep appointments for formal-wear fittings.
- Assist in planning and financing the bachelor party.

- Attend the rehearsal and rehearsal dinner.
- Distribute wedding programs.
- Make certain that family members have their corsages or boutonnieres.
- Seat guests.
- Escort bridesmaids during the recessional.
- Collect any personal items left by guests at the ceremony.
- Mingle and dance at the reception.

TRADITIONAL EXPENSES FOR THE GROOMSMEN & USHERS

- *Personal wedding formal wear*
- *Personal travel expenses*
- *Personal hotel accommodations*

A NEW TWIST ON TRADITION

I will never forget the look on my aunt's face when I informed her of my wife's decision to forgo a band or a DJ for our wedding reception (a decision I fully agreed with, by the way).

After considerable thought, we had determined that the popular trend of using a preselected song list stored on our iPod would not only ensure all of our favorite and most meaningful songs would be played during the reception, it also would provide a cost-effective alternative music provider. Although initially skeptical and altogether confused about what this iPod thing was, my aunt danced just the same at our reception. And so did everyone else.

When it comes to respecting tradition while embracing change, one way for a savvy groom-in-training to straddle the fine line between the two is to remember that as a general rule, regardless of how much tradition may cramp your style, some wedding customs aren't going anywhere anytime soon. So in general, if it's steeped in tradition, respect it.

For instance, no matter how you approach the formation of your bridal party, there is very little wiggle room when it comes to structuring the roles and responsibilities played by respective members of the bridal party. Overall, it's a cast of characters that can serve a bride and groom well.

But while this tradition doesn't warrant a change in and of itself, the way in which it is managed could use a fresh approach. One of the biggest mistakes made by the novice groom is expecting his best man, groomsmen, and ushers to somehow magically know what is expected of them. Even worse, though his guys may initially have been informed of all that is required, the groom frequently and foolishly expects them to remember it! This is a big mistake.

In a nutshell, groomsmen aren't bridesmaids.

The modern groom can take a new approach that helps reduce wedding-day blunders and pre-wedding stress: treat his groomsmen like workers on a construction site for which he is the foreman. If his men are in order, informed, and in step, the wedding day will go much more smoothly.

To find other ways to think outside the box, consider ideas other couples have had that have balanced tradition with modernity. You might be a rookie at getting married yourself, but you've probably attended a hefty number of weddings in your lifetime. It might seem like common sense, but one of the biggest mistakes fledgling grooms make is failing to apply new ideas to their planning that they've already seen work elsewhere.

I'm not saying you need to produce a wealth of original ideas that will dazzle brides everywhere. Throughout the labored process of planning my wedding, there were numerous occasions where I helped my fiancée overcome planning hitches by simply borrowing ideas from other weddings I had attended. At my best friend's wedding, for example, he and his wife had their engagement photo blown up large enough for all guests in attendance to sign and inscribe with good wishes. I knew even before their wedding cake was cut that I just had to rip off this really cool idea.

As it turns out, there's nothing quite like a brilliant idea borrowed to help the smart groom solve his bride's planning dilemmas. Scores of such examples have been left by the ghosts of grooms past that can be used to the benefit of today's marrying man.

HERE'S TO THE BRIDE & GROOM!

Famously Quotable Wedding & Marriage Quips

- *"They say love is blind and that marriage is an institution. So, in other words, marriage is an institution for the blind." - Mae West*

- *"Getting married for sex is like buying a 747 for the free peanuts" - Jeff Foxworthy*

- *"I was married by a judge. I should have asked for a jury." - Groucho Marx*

- *"The best way to remember your wife's birthday is to forget it once." - H.V. Prochnow*

- *"I have learned that only two things are necessary to keep one's wife happy. First, let her think she's having her own way. And second, let her have it." -Lyndon B. Johnson*

- *"My husband and I divorced over religious differences. He thought he was God, and I didn't." -Unknown*

- *"My wife and I were happy for twenty years. Then we met." - Rodney Dangerfield*

- *"I haven't spoken to my wife in years. I didn't want to interrupt her." - Rodney Dangerfield*

- *"Marriage has no guarantees. If that's what you're looking for, go live with a car battery." - Erma Bombeck*

Chapter 4

The Big Stuff

Although there are many details and responsibilities that will be addressed before the big day, for now we're going to concentrate on the exceptionally important tasks that are the most cumbersome and time consuming of all the challenges ahead. This journey begins with the lifeblood of your wedding: the budget.

Paying for a Priceless Wedding

There comes a point in every wedding budget plan when the groom can't help but wonder if he and his bride will have to sell sex tapes from their honeymoon just to break even on the enormous financial obligation they incurred in planning the wedding.

You can take some comfort in knowing that the overwhelming majority of couples squander big bucks simply through the improper management of their wedding budget. Many brides and grooms, in fact, start cutting checks even before determining the size of the pool of funds from which they will draw throughout the planning process.

Don't make that potentially destructive mistake. The reason a great number of weddings get postponed has nothing to do with the bride or groom rethinking their marriage plans. Instead, the ceremonies are delayed because the financial well ran dry.

Just consciously acknowledging how much money you presently have can be a deciding factor in just how soon you can afford to set a date. For this reason, right after the question is popped and the parents are notified, create a spreadsheet—either electronically or on an old-fashioned piece of paper. Together, begin listing as many wedding-related expenses as you can imagine.

In examining relevant expenses, take care to catalog every service or product you want and their corresponding costs. Make your spreadsheet all-inclusive—that is, allow space to note the dates of any monies due, deposits paid, and outstanding expenses yet to be determined.

Don't panic when some of your expenses go astray. You can always reallocate money from one expense to another if need be. Most wedding budgets aren't met perfectly. In fact, the majority go over budget (although only slightly). The important thing to remember is that your budget will never get too far out of whack as long as you keep a close watch on your pennies during this wallet-draining phase.

Another important tip to remember is that your budget sheet shouldn't include only the major expenses (reception venue, florist, caterer, etc.). Nine times out of ten, wedding budgets go wrong by thousands of dollars as a result of not factoring in all the minor expenses. Be mindful to include fields to track the little things, like postage for invitations, private security for the reception, and even gratuity payments to bartenders, hairdressers, catering staff, and other vendors.

Once you've amassed a list of everything you'll need and the bucks you'll require to bankroll your event, not only will you have the beginnings of a financial plan, you will also have a fairly accurate estimate of the total cost of your wedding.

THE BANQUET HALL IS TAKEN? THERE'S ALWAYS "HOOTERS"

You and your bride are likely to discover very quickly just how busy the wedding market is, particularly when it comes to selecting a ceremony site and reception venue. If her heart is set on one location and you discover it's already taken, whatever you do, don't shrug it off and recommend someplace stupid. Brides take the place and time of their weddings very seriously.

Unfortunately, many women who've had a late start in planning or a short engagement are forced to choose their second or third preference. Be sensitive to her dilemma, and quietly realize to yourself that in no time at all, she'll likely be pleased with the new venue and all will be right with the world again.

Now, if you're planning a wedding twelve to twenty-four months ahead of time, there should be little difficulty (if any) in reserving the facilities you want on the dates you need them. Then again, if you're like most couples and plan your wedding only six to twelve months ahead of time, it may be considerably more difficult to get first dibs on your preferred site selections. With millions of Americans walking down the aisle each year, there's an excellent chance you've already been beaten to the punch for reservations on the last Saturday in June at the cute little church only a few miles from your home.

On the other hand, even if you're planning a wedding on short notice, you can still pull it off, as long as you remain flexible on the date and venue. Many couples who have been devastated to learn their desired wedding date at their chosen location was already taken, ended up saving money by going against the grain of established tradition and rethinking their choices. For example, each year, thousands of couples marry on a weeknight instead of a weekend. Not only are the prices for wedding-related services during non-peak times cheaper, they are also more readily accessible. And if you're willing to buck seasonal traditions, the sky's the limit for your wedding planning.

In the big picture, though, it is most important for you to reserve facilities as quickly as possible. When doing so, however, give some consideration to the convenience of those you plan to invite. Even though this wedding is about you and your bride and you're willing to get creative about securing your venue, there's a strong possibility that many of your guests will be coming from far and wide to attend the ceremony. As a result, a weeknight wedding might preclude many willing guests from being able to attend. Likewise, if your hearts aren't powerfully set on one particular location as of yet, remember that securing something centrally located will help accommodate as many guests as possible.

If time and flexibility permit, it also can be polite (and ultimately in your own best interests) to consult your closest family and friends about the wedding date you have in mind, especially potential bridal party members. Although you can't plan your wedding around one hundred different individual schedules, it would be a good idea to confirm that your potential best man hasn't already booked a nonrefundable vacation at Disney World during the weekend you want to get married.

You Invited WHO?!?!

The process of narrowing a long list of potential invitees down to a smaller list is stressful enough to make anyone seriously consider calling the whole thing off. Six months before our wedding, my personal list of family and friends amounted to more than sixty names. This was particularly problematic given that my fiancée and her large family had not yet turned in their list, and we initially planned (flippantly, that is) to have only a total of one hundred guests at our wedding. Although these tense moments led to our individual rants about how the "other side" wanted to dominate the guest list, the truth was that we each shared equal blame for causing such strife in the first place. By not setting a firm guest maximum and providing comparable invites limits for each side of the family, we were ultimately just asking for drama.

No matter the size of your wedding, establishing the guest list begins with placing a ceiling on the total number of guests you want or can afford to have in attendance. Even if money and/or space don't dictate your number, try to set a reasonable estimate before you put so much as a single name on paper.

Since you, your parents, your bride, and her parents will likely be adamant about inviting certain people, divvy up the guest list into fair portions (preferably equal) for both sides of the family. While still honoring your initial cap, let everyone have a certain number of guests of their own choosing. Although it is normal for whoever is financing the wedding to feel entitled to determine a greater chunk of the guest list, try to tone down any such expectations (if possible) for the sake of equality in the division of the list.

For many couples, this process simply doesn't go smoothly. Much of the time, the bickering among warring factions of friends and family influences the bride and groom to amend their guest list and increase their budget, putting them in a precarious position.

Many families struggling with the division of the guest list come up with other criteria for determining who should and shouldn't be invited. For example, you could limit invitees to only those with whom *both* the bride and groom are familiar. This can reduce a lot of ancillary guests that slant the list too heavily toward one half of the couple.

An equally nerve-wracking aspect of creating the guest list is staying on top of all the changes along the way. Prior to my cousin's wedding a few years ago, I thought I could hear his fiancée screaming from nearly seven hundred miles away when she learned he had lost "the master list." Even though my cousin is a computer whiz with more desktops than friends, it never occurred to him that he should open a spreadsheet (remember the budgeting process?) and maintain a running tally of who was invited and who was coming.

If you do create a spreadsheet (as successful grooms do), you can use it to record more than just the names of the individuals who survived the chopping block. Include fields for mailing addresses and for the number of guests your invitees are planning on bringing. As a general rule, invited couples aren't given a "plus one" option; unmarried guests, however, should be afforded an opportunity to bring a guest with them. Few prospective attendees, after all, will want to come to a wedding alone and without someone to dance with, especially if they don't know a lot of people at your wedding. Similarly, don't forget that vendors have to eat too. If you're going to have a photographer and videographer, for example, be sure to add two more to your running head count.

If done correctly, a single Excel file will keep you

very well organized for when the time finally comes (and it will come sooner than you think) to snail mail the invitations.

A THEME? WHAT THEME?

In the past, selecting a style or theme for a wedding meant determining how formal or casual the wedding would be. Although these questions remain essential and require a decision early on in the planning stages, the idea of a wedding "theme" has evolved considerably in recent years.

Gone are the days when the wedding was its own theme. Modern weddings have increasingly come to employ fanciful themes intending to transport the bride, groom, and all guests in attendance to a whimsical place within the bride's own colorful imagination.

From winter wonderland themes to Victorian settings, there is no shortage of ideas for your bride to explore. Imagine frolicking in an enchanted forest beneath a starry sky. Or running through an open field chasing butterflies amid a sunlit landscape.

Themes come in all varieties. Take the 1998 wedding of TV personality Melissa Rivers and horse breeder John Endicott. Held at the Plaza Hotel in New York City, the famed million dollar wedding (paid for by Melissa's mom, legendary entertainer Joan Rivers), was a gala more elaborate than a presidential inauguration. As one account gushed: "The outstretched branches of one hundred white birch trees arched over the aisle as the bride made her entrance in the Terrace Room of the Plaza Hotel, where three hundred and fifty attendees witnessed the exchange of vows in a winter wonderland filled with 25,000 white roses, hydrangeas, and lilies of the valley."

Wedding themes have become so popular, in fact, that many couples now think a traditional wedding is dated and unimaginative. Nothing could be further from the truth. A theme is an addition to the occasion, not an essential ingredient. Anyone who tells you otherwise probably has a financial stake in helping you adopt an elaborate theme for your wedding.

To be fair, themes can provide a lovely punctuation mark on what will hopefully be a beautiful occasion. Just don't let yourself or your bride get carried away with the notion that a wedding theme has to be overpowering. A simple coordinated color scheme for everything from the formal wear down to the centerpieces could very well constitute a theme. At the end of the day, you need to have the wedding that you and your bride want, not the wedding that bridal magazines, wedding planners, and overzealous friends and relatives demand you have.

If you're going to have a theme, you'll need to decide on it well before the menu, flowers, music, or even the invitations have been selected. As you consider potential concepts, be careful to choose a theme that suits your personalities. Even though this decision typically rests with the bride, it helps for the groom to be in sync with her decision. After all, whether the affair is formal and sophisticated or simple and casual, you will have to orient yourself, your decisions, and your actions to suit the occasion.

Selecting a particular theme will guide you and your bride's decisions in the months to follow. From choosing the menu to selecting party favors, important details will hinge on the theme. After you decide (or, more likely, are told) what your wedding will look like, you can concentrate your efforts on the choices, purchases, and creations necessary to bring to life whatever vivid fantasies are envisioned for your wedding day.

FEEDING THE FLOCK

As guests descend on your ceremony site, two things will begin happening simultaneously. First, they will blissfully share in your glorious moment of happiness and possibly will weep with joy at the beautiful union taking place before their watery eyes. Second, they will get hungry.

In the coming months, you and your bride will struggle to orchestrate the most aesthetically pleasing ceremony and reception you are personally and financially capable of pulling off. And although many of your guests will certainly lose their breaths over the dazzling centerpieces or ice sculptures awaiting their arrival, the majority will care only about (and remember) one element of your reception: the food.

To be sure, the quality of music, ambience, and company are very important and in fact utterly vital in transforming an ordinary wedding reception into an all-out party for the ages. But there's nothing like good food to make a wedding, or bad food to break it.

When you start planning the reception menu, consider your theme. Selecting menu items will be a lot easier this way. After all, if your reception is Italian themed, there's a good chance you'll know better than to select egg rolls for the buffet. Keeping the style of your wedding in mind during the menu selection process should dramatically simplify your quest for the ideal wedding meal.

Many wedding planners urge even couples on a shoe-string budget to put the full weight of their funds behind dinner. If this means having fewer floral arrangements, so be it. Don't skimp on the food if at all possible.

When it comes to weddings, there's very little gray area in terms of the quality of the meal provided. It tends to be either among the best meals you've had in a while, or the worst. Many factors, however, can have an influence on which side of this equation your wedding meal falls. If, for instance, you reserve a banquet hall that provides dinner (and prohibits you from having it catered by another vendor) you have no choice but to select items from the menu available. On the other hand, if you're able to choose your own meal provider, allot considerably more time to this decision.

As with any product or service, it's never a bad idea to ask for referrals from friends and family members who have recently—and I stress recently—been through the same motions in a wedding of their own. If your goal is to still have guests talking about how good the food was by the time your tenth wedding anniversary rolls around, it's a good idea to take referrals seriously, from both people you know and from the vendors themselves. Couples without a healthy reserve of recommendations can always contact the International Caterers Association (www.icacater.org) or the National Association of Catering Executives (www.nace.net) for a list of licensed caterers in their area.

Inevitably, you will meet with several potential candidates face to apron. If you're the one charged with vetting the contending caterers, here are some helpful questions to ask that will not only get to the heart of your concerns and ensure a successful meal, but also will impress the garter right off your bride!

- Given the style of my wedding, which menu items would you recommend?
- Are there any menu items that you specialize in?
- Taking the size of our guest list into account, what would be the cost-per-person?
- Does the dinner cost-per-person cover meals only, or are other expenses (staff, linens, gratuity, etc.) also included?
- What is the size of your serving staff? How many prep cooks? And what will be their attire?
- Is there a discounted charge for children's meals?

- What vegetarian options are available for guests that can't eat meat?

- Are appetizers appropriate for the occasion? If so, how would they be served and what menu options are suitable?

- How much more is the cost per person of a sit-down dinner relative to the cost per person of a buffet style meal?

- Are there service costs beyond the per-person meal expense? Is setup and cleanup included in the package price?

- How much time is required for setup and cleanup?

- Are you a licensed caterer?

- Do you have a liquor license?

- If we want to provide our own champagne for the toast, or even all the alcohol for the reception, do you charge a corkage or service fee?

- How many other weddings will you be servicing the same week or weekend as mine?

- Do you provide silverware, serving pieces, decorative items, glasses, tables, chairs, etc.?

- If these accessories are available, what variety of colors and styles can be selected?

- Will you be the individual assigned to my wedding? (If not, make arrangements to meet personally with whoever will be on site at your wedding.)

- Can you provide a wedding cake? If not, do you charge a cake cutting and service fee if we provide a cake from another vendor?

- When is the absolute latest we can provide a revised or final head count?

- May I please have a copy of your standard contract?

- What is the deposit required to reserve your services for our wedding date? When will the remaining balance be due?

- Can you provide a list of recent referrals as well as photographs from recent events you've catered?

Just as one would advise you to shop around before making any enormous purchase (which, essentially, a caterer is), be sure to contact a variety of potential candidates, obtain price lists, check availability, and, most important, make arrangements to meet personally with each vendor to ask questions and sample their work—undoubtedly the best part of the process! Leave no questions unanswered and no details to chance.

If a particular caterer strikes your fancy, really get to know the man or woman behind the apron. What does he or she do best, buffets or sit-down dinners? Naturally, savvy caterers will tell you that they can do either equally well. Much of the time, this isn't true. If your caterer is a gourmet chef who, according to their portfolio, prepares sit-down meals and buffet dinners at a ten-to-one ratio, there's a great possibility that you can bank on a better sit-down meal than a buffet style dinner. You also will likely encounter caterers for whom the opposite is true. Be mindful to select a caterer that won't be out of his element on your wedding day because of your needs or your budget. There are a million caterers to choose from. All are hungry for your business. The right one for you is out there somewhere!

THE WEDDING CAKE

As the old joke goes, a dietician was once addressing a large audience.

"The crap we put into our bodies is enough to kill some people," the dietician said. "Red meat is awful. Soft drinks erode your stomach lining. Chinese food is loaded with MSG. Vegetables are covered in pesticides, and none of us realizes the long-term harm caused by the germs in our drinking water.

"But there is one thing that is the most dangerous of all, and we all have eaten it, or will. Can anyone here tell me which food causes the most grief and suffering for years after eating it?"

A seventy-five-year-old man in the front row stood up and said, "Wedding cake."

Although there are millions of happily married men who can disprove this, there are considerably fewer who can honestly say that the selection of a wedding cake is a pleasant experience.

Ironically, all the ingredients—if you'll pardon the pun—point to a remarkably enjoyable endeavor. I mean, you get to go bakery-hopping all over town to sample free servings of the finest cakes you will ever taste in your entire life. What's not to like? But at some point, almost every groom tagging along in the wedding-cake selection process will begin referring to this sweet staple as "the damn wedding cake." Why? Because the appearance of the cake can be to your bride one of the biggest and more crucial decisions of your entire wedding plan. At some point, it's only natural for a frustrated groom to develop the urge to shout "It's just a cake! Pick one!"

As we've said, it's vital to not rush your fiancée, especially when it comes to a major decision. In this regard, I completely lucked out during the planning of my own wedding. Our hometown banquet facility not only offered onsite catering, they also provided an array of gorgeous wedding cakes to choose among.

Although there is virtually no chance of your bride delegating the selection of your wedding cake to you alone, it is still in your best interest to tag along and participate in the choosing. If anything, perhaps you can help narrow the choices by proactively soliciting referrals, to limit the number of potential bakeries to a reasonable quantity.

When it comes to "reasonable," however, it's unlikely you'll be able to apply that word to the price of a wedding cake. The average cake ranges in price from ten to fifteen dollars per slice! This is due to the fact that searching for a "wedding cake" automatically increases the price dramatically. An ordinary sheet cake large enough to feed your guests would be considerably less expensive. But if you or your bride is set on the traditional, grandiose mountain of beautifully adorned decadent icing surrounding a behemoth cake, there are few inexpensive substitutes.

One possible suggestion, however, is to attend local bridal shows and keep your eyes peeled for ambitious young culinary students distributing business cards offering their reduced-rate services. Prior to our wedding, my fiancée and I were inundated with similar opportunities within the first ten minutes of a sparsely attended bridal expo. Whether it's for extra money or extra credit, there are up-and-coming bakery chefs looking for opportunities. If you know of a regional culinary school in your neck of the woods, it might be worth your while to place an inquiry.

Keep in mind that nobody is twisting your arm to have a particular kind of wedding cake. In fact, a significant number of wedding planners have begun advising clients to serve alternative desserts, like mini pastries, in the shape of a wedding cake. No matter what you choose, just play it safe and opt for an established business with plenty of samples to share. Be sure to discuss with your cake provider any details or expenses beyond the design and preparation. From the delivery of the cake to the distribution of the slices, find out if the bakery staff will take care of everything, or if the caterer needs to be notified to round up his staff for this job. As always, discuss the payment plan and read the contract a few times before signing. Make sure that your final order is itemized on the contract with all charges for fillings, delivery, decorations, et cetera included.

As an expert groom (at least by the time of the wedding), be certain to personally tend to your wife and ensure that she gets to eat a piece of the cake on your actual wedding. My wife and I were so excited and hectic at our reception that we didn't get any cake except for the little we shoved into one another's faces during the cutting. To make matters worse, we violated the longstanding tradition of freezing the top tier of the wedding cake and saving it to be eaten on the first anniversary—Christa and I didn't make it through the first week of our marriage before the top tier of our cake was gone. Learning afterwards from friends who recalled how gross their year-old freezer burned cake tasted, we felt better about our judgment to eat the cake while it was still as fresh on our minds as it was in storage.

OK, WHO GOT GRANDMA DRUNK?

There's nothing like having an overserved friend, relative, or wedding crasher upstage the show, embarrass family and friends, and humiliate himself—right along with the bride and groom.

It's no secret that weddings provide the perfect opportunity to celebrate a happy occasion with a drink… or twelve. But awkward moments usually accompany such intoxicated behavior and can seriously disrupt or destroy an otherwise pleasant affair. As the groom, it is especially appropriate for you to take proactive measures to prevent a booze breakdown at your wedding.

When it comes to serving alcohol at the reception, be careful to really weigh your options. Despite what you may have read or been told elsewhere, there are no rules about how much or what types of alcohol you should serve, or even that alcohol has to be served in the first place. Understandably, you don't want to punish all of your guests just to keep under control the few loose cannons that might overdo it at the bar. But you still need to be extraordinarily vigilant about your choices regarding alcohol.

On one hand, keeping your guests well hydrated on feel-good juice can be a nice thank-you gesture, particularly for individuals who have traveled a great distance or given a wonderful gift. For this reason, conventional wisdom frowns upon having a cash bar at a wedding. On the other hand, if you are inclined to believe that certain individuals in attendance may abuse this expensive privilege, it might be in the best interest of your party, everyone's safety, and your wallet to make guests pay for their own alcohol. Of course, soft drinks, coffee, and other nonalcoholic drinks should remain on your tab.

If you're like most couples, you're probably not going to want a dry wedding. So if the bubbly will be flowing, the first step in stocking the bar is to speak with your caterer, venue manager, or hired bartender about the number of guests you're expecting and the types of drinks you want to have. This will give him or her an idea of the volume of alcohol needed. Next, you'll want to explore the costs associated with the options available to you. Are you charged per drink, or is a package deal on the booze available? This is an important question, particularly if you're planning to offer mixed drinks in addition to beer and wine.

Once you've determined the alcohol you need and provided for adequate security (usually an off-duty police officer or other professional security guard), your next step is to decide on the availability of the alcohol. That is, will the bar be open from the start of the reception until the end? Or will you opt for limited bar hours? Many couples prefer to have the bar open at the start of the reception and then closed during dinner. Typically, the bar is then reopened for a few hours or until the end of the party. Another option is to have the bar open for the first few hours of the reception and then close it for the rest of the night. Your bandleader or DJ can announce bar hours at the start of the reception to prevent any tempers from flaring once the bar closes.

A predetermined window of opportunity for drinking is an ideal way to reduce the possibility of someone having a drunken rampage just about the time you're trying to concentrate on the chicken dance. Of course, if you're uncomfortable about completely cutting everyone off, you can close the bar but still have alcohol available. That is, you can direct the wait staff to maneuver through the crowd and take drink orders once the bar is closed.

Although you may think this isn't a very effective strategy for cooling consumption, open bar access is far more likely to get people drunk faster.

If your goal is to provide as much booze as your guests desire, there are very few decisions you need to make, apart from determining how many bar stations to have so that guests won't have to wait to be served. However, if your intent it to limit alcohol consumption, then reducing access, service, and the availability of certain types of alcohol are your first lines of defense.

Ultimately, no matter how vigilant you are prior to your guest's arrival, if someone is hell-bent on getting blasted, there's a good chance they're going to. Since you and your bride will have your hands full and hopefully will be enjoying the occasion, don't count on yourself or the security guard (who will typically intervene only once disaster has struck) to monitor drinking habits at your wedding reception. If there was ever an appropriate time to put your best man or groomsmen to work, it's at the reception. Although they are likely to be having a good time too, ask that they serve as monitors for potential drunk people. Bartenders should be expected to limit service to the overserved, but they don't always come through. A designated point person to chaperone drinkers is ultimately the most effective way to keep drinking under control.

It also never hurts to make arrangements for a consistent stream of after-wedding snacks to be provided. Since food is an effective means for absorbing alcohol in one's stomach (and, consequently, reducing its effects) offer some non-salty snacks that can curb alcohol overindulgence. In addition, with hydration itself serving as a great aid to sobriety, have nonalcoholic drinks readily available at tables and bar stations for the duration of your wedding reception.

If Murphy's Law somehow still visits your wedding the way it does millions of others, be sure to personally or by proxy (again, a good job for the best man or groomsmen) arrange for a cab or even a hotel room for guests who may think they can drive home but most likely shouldn't.

Having witnessed a close friend mourn the death of a relative who was killed in an automobile accident following his wedding, I can't possibly stress enough the value of keeping everyone happy but safe on the joyous occasion of your wedding.

FOCUSING ON THE PHOTOGRAPHER

Less than six weeks before our wedding, I received a call from the photographer whose services I had reserved a long time earlier. Claiming that a "medical emergency" would preclude him from shooting our wedding, my fiancée and I were left stranded without a photographer.

Stricken with panic after being rejected by every other photographer I could find by frantically searching the yellow pages, we actually began discussing the possibility of having one of our family members or friends take photos with our digital camera. This was a last resort we had never anticipated confronting.

Luckily, shortly after getting the bombshell news from our ailing photographer (although the cynic in me wonders if he was really ill), one of my recently published books received a mention in the entertainment column of one of our local newspapers. The story detailed my busy schedule as an author, and mentioned that I was also a groom in search of a photographer.

Incredibly, the article sparked a wave of phone and emails to the newspaper. Within hours, I found myself swimming in names and numbers of amateur and professional photographers looking to shoot my wedding. Although a number of potential candidates were simply trying to take advantage of the situation by charging a small fortune, others were as kind and sympathetic as they were talented.

From the precipice of disaster came a regional photographer who was scheduled to return from a gig in the Bahamas only hours before our wedding. Despite his hectic schedule, bustling portfolio, and talents that far superseded our modest little ceremony, he not only made himself available to rescue our photographer-less wedding, he gave us a better package deal than any other photographer we had contacted.

In hindsight, his sincerity, talent, and professionalism were matched only by his photography of our wedding. Unfortunately, not all crises are resolved so beautifully, and not all photographers are like ours.

In several critical ways, the search for a great photographer parallels the search for other important wedding vendors. First, get as many references as possible. The phone book doesn't count—it's an inventory, not a filtered list of quality names. Second, contact as many recommended candidates as possible to check availability. Finally, meet personally with each not only to discuss prices and packages, but to get a sense of whether this professional is a good fit for your wedding.

When it comes to your photographer, there is one critical factor that ranks just as highly as the quality of their portfolio and the strength of their recommendations: their personality.

Ordinarily, a pleasant demeanor in a vendor is an advantage, but not a requirement. With a wedding photographer, however, the personality behind the lens is vitally important to the entire process. Why? Because there is no vendor you and your guests will spend as much time with on the wedding day as the photographer. No one wants an uptight, self-important windbag bossing around guests and the bridal party to achieve his own ostentatious vision. Temperamental or arrogant photographers—despite their obvious talents—are inclined to make weddings more about themselves than their subjects.

You can generally tell from your first encounter with a professional photographer if his or her personality mixes well with yours and your bride's. If you think you're going to be uncomfortable or put off in any way by this person on your wedding day, discount every recommendation heard and photo album you've perused and mosey on down the line to the next name on your list. Continue the process of elimination until you find a photographer with whom you could comfortably hang out for the day. Essentially, this is what you and your wedding party will do.

Once you've narrowed the field, get down to business. Don't waste time asking questions about the photographer's equipment, lights, and other technical aspects. If this person has come highly recommended, presents an impressive body of work, and mixes well with you and your bride, there's an exceptional possibility that your would-be photographer wields the proper tools of the trade. Instead, focus on the service and scheduling components of your working relationship.

Some important questions to ask:

- How many hours are included in your service?
- Will you bring an assistant to the ceremony and reception?
- Are your photos shot digitally or on film?
- Approximately how many photos do you expect to shoot throughout the course of the day?
- How long after the wedding will we receive the proofs?
- Will proofs be delivered in print or digitally?
- Is a wedding album included, or is that purchased at additional cost?
- How much do you charge for prints?
- Do we retain reprint rights to the photos, or must we always order prints from you?

Based on your situation, other questions may also be important. Don't forget, however, to let the photographer ask some questions too. To assist his efforts as much as possible, provide a comprehensive outline of the day's time line. This will enable your photographer to plan for the shots he will need to take and the equipment he will need accessible.

In addition, many couples take into consideration the layout of their church and reception site and request a mandatory walk-through with their photographer either at the rehearsal or on another mutually convenient occasion. Brides worry that an overzealous photographer in the aisle will somehow impede everyone's gaze as she makes her grand entrance. Such concerns aren't altogether without merit. For this reason, it's essential to have a serious discussion with your photographer about just how aggressive or involved he will be during critical moments of the day's festivities.

When you're looking to cut costs and corners, its easy to think that a photographer's assistant is unnecessary, an extra expense, or just a sign of a lethargic photographer. Nothing could be further from the truth. Most wedding planners, in fact, would advise against hiring any professional photographer that doesn't employ one or more assistants. After all, the last thing you want is a great photo opportunity lost because your photographer was taking a bathroom break or couldn't find the proper lens. An assistant is truly an invaluable benefit and a sign of a fantastic professional photographer.

At the end of the day, be sure to respect your photographer, his staff, and his work. This means also treating the professional as a person. From ensuring that he and his assistant are fed to making proper arrangements for timely compensation, place a premium on the value of a good wedding photographer and act accordingly. After all, your wedding photos are probably going to be prominently featured throughout your home for decades to come. When you think of it this way, a wedding photographer's fee is really a small price to pay for captured memories that will last and be cherished for a lifetime.

AMATEUR HOUR

No matter how superb your photographer is, there's a recurring truth at weddings: some of the best photos are shot by amateurs—that is, your barely sober relatives and friends. It's not a bad idea to put disposable cameras at every table. It's a great way to ensure that no spontaneous moments will be missed. Also don't forget to ask guests to email their digital photos to you after the wedding. Chances are, these candid shots will hold you over until the professional ones turn up.

DJ or Band? An Epic Struggle

Without exception, music and weddings are inextricably linked. There is nothing like good music to set the mood for the occasion and truly make the party a sensation.

The overwhelming majority of couples have but three options for providing music at their wedding reception: a band, a DJ, or an iPod.

Traditionally, DJs receive more business than bands at wedding receptions because a DJ can offer a much broader variety of music than your average local band. The benefits to hiring a DJ include the ability to:

- Choose from thousands of original songs capable of pleasing guests of all ages, including requests
- Play music without breaks or interruption throughout the entire evening
- Provide running commentary and quips as called for throughout the night
- Change tempo readily when the mood or reception activity calls for it
- Provide more hours of entertainment at a considerably lower price than a band
- Adjust the music volume as requested

When speaking with DJs that either have been recommended or heavily advertised, be certain you're not hiring a showman. There's noting worse than a DJ who thinks he's personally hosting your wedding and consistently tries to steal the show with his overpowering personality and cheesy (and maybe inappropriate) humor. Conversely, booking a DJ who simply changes CDs throughout the night without any personality isn't ideal either. Find one who offers a healthy balance between adding personality to the occasion and allowing the music to remain the central focus of the reception.

If you hire a DJ, provide him or her with a list of names and corresponding pronunciations if necessary. When the time comes for introductions or announcements, you don't want your DJ resembling the guy from the famous commercial where "Mr. Dumas" is referred to as "Mr. Dumb Ass."

Similarly, give your DJ a "must play" list and a "do not play" list. By personally meeting with your DJ prior to the wedding, you can ensure that he or she has the music you want, including the specific songs you'd like for your first dance, garter throw, cake cutting, et cetera. Although you can't possibility orchestrate an entire playlist for your DJ to follow, you can certainly establish parameters and provide guidance.

If you're leaning toward having a live band at your wedding, there probably will be a number of guests excited about your decision. Since there is truly nothing like live music, a band can quickly inspire people to hit the dance floor, whereas a DJ could take a while to get the crowd warmed up. Live bands:

- Usually provide better sound quality than a DJ
- Help complete a wedding theme, especially if a particular genre of music is best suited for your theme (a 1950s era wedding style, for example, can come to life with a band that plays mostly '50s music).
- Change the tempo of the dancing and mood of the floor as desired at any given time.
- Energize a crowd better than prerecorded music could.

Unfortunately, a leading reason why bands tend to lose a significant amount of business to DJs is because live bands are often inordinately expensive. Rarely can you find a decent band that charges less than two thousand dollars. The lion's share of quality wedding bands charge anywhere from five to ten thousand dollars and up for just one evening of live music.

While cost can obviously be a prohibitive factor for some, others are generally concerned with the fact that bands can't provide music constantly. Naturally, musicians are human beings that require food, oxygen, and rest like everyone else. And even though you can always put on a CD to fill in during the interim while the band breaks, that often effects a noticeable and sudden change in the reception's atmosphere.

For a lot of couples, the epic struggle that is deciding between a band and DJ rages on for months. Both sides present valid merits. Yet, at the end of the day, remember that if you know a great band you truly believe would be a fantastic addition to your wedding, book them and forget about the DJs you've met. Likewise, it's always better to side with a DJ when you just can't make up your mind about a band. In this case, it's far better to be safe than sorry.

Despite heavily weighing the pros and cons of each, if a DJ doesn't strike your fancy and the band just can't make the cut, keep in mind that there remains a third option available, a contemporary trend known as the "iPod wedding."

When my fiancée and I decided against having a live band or a DJ, we spent weeks compiling the perfect playlist for our wedding. Since our reception site came equipped with speakers and a soundboard for prerecorded music, we simply input the music from our iPod into the mixer, and we ended up with a customized "DJ" that was better received by our guests than we could possibly have imagined. Best of all, we delegated the introduction duties to a close family friend who did a much better job than any unfamiliar DJ could have.

Surely, iPod weddings aren't for everyone. But they are perfect for some. If you can't settle the epic struggle that is picking a DJ or a band (or if your entertainment has an emergency cancellation) the iPod is more than a last resort. It's a personalized presentation of meaningful music that can run the gamut of emotions you hope to be felt on your wedding day.

HYDRANGEAS COST WHAT?!?!

Unlike certain wedding vendors (photographers, caterers, DJs, etc.) florists are ubiquitous. In other words, you won't have trouble finding a variety of potential florists to choose among. Complicating matters some is the fact that a majority will likely come highly recommended. If so, you'll have to base your eventual decision on other factors beside word of mouth.

Selecting the right florist for you begins with visiting numerous floral shops around town without an initial appointment. Your first visit should be unannounced and does not require any professional consultation. You are simply there to get a feel for the store and the types of arrangements on display throughout the shop. You can generally surmise, based on your initial read of the place, if this florist is right for you. By now, your bride will probably have visualized the floral arrangements she wants. If nothing similar jumps out at her during a visit, which will surely include perusing books of floral samples, it's time to move on to the next shop.

Every step of the way, take care to examine both the arrangements on display and those found in the florist's portfolio. Be mindful of the age of the photos provided. Are they out of style, or contemporary? Do the flowers around the shop and in photographs look fresh, or are there brown, wilted edges surrounding the petals? It's incredible how much you can learn about a florist from one simple visit to their flower shop.

Once you've found a few florists you are interested in, make appointments to consult with the owner. Discuss your vision, your concerns, your budget, et cetera. This is a great opportunity to measure how interested the florist is in your wedding. You may think that all florists want whatever business they can get. But in truth, not everybody is as professional or passionate about his or her craft as you would hope. And when it comes to wedding flowers, expertise shows.

As the groom along for consultation (it's unlikely you'll be flying solo on this mission), take note of how engaged the florist is in your bride's ideas for floral arrangements. Many florists are divas who will only do for your wedding what they think they should. This is an immediate red flag. Naturally, it's one thing to take professional consultation into consideration when selecting wedding flowers, but it's another to dramatically overhaul your vision because a florist supposedly knows better.

Don't fool yourself. Flowers are enormously expensive. I myself initially suffered from hydrangea sticker shock. But my fiancée and I eventually found the right florist who wasn't hell-bent on her own vision and determined to squeeze every penny from us. Keep searching until you find a florist that meshes with your personalities and your vision for the wedding. The process of selecting (and paying for) flowers can be exhaustive, but you don't have to break the bank by any stretch of the imagination.

When visiting florists, it's always helpful to bring photos of the flowers that you and your bride want for the wedding. Whether you've downloaded images online or plucked a few flowers right from the ground, be sure your florist adequately understands the look you're going for. Since your technical knowledge of horticulture probably will be limited in comparison, don't rely on your descriptions of flowers to express your wishes. Such description can easily be misinterpreted.

If already determined, share with the florist your color scheme, as well as photos of the ceremony and reception sites. It can even prove beneficial to show snapshots of the bridal gown and selected formal wear. Last, provide a complete list of the sum total of flowers and arrangements you will need, taking note of who they are for so that the florist can label corsages, boutonnieres, et cetera with the proper names.

As you inch toward a final decision on whom to entrust with the floral duties, continue to ask pertinent questions about the specifics relating to your occasion. For example:

- Were the flowers on display in your store arranged by the same person who will arrange our flowers?
- Are there delivery, setup, or rental fees?
- What's the very latest we can change our order if we come up with a new idea?
- Can you put the itemized listing (with descriptions), the name of our floral designer, and the estimated delivery times in the contract?
- Which flowers that we're considering will be in season during our wedding?
- Have you ever provided flowers at our church or reception site?
- Will the flowers be delivered, or will we have to pick them up?
- If they are delivered, how early will you need access to the church and reception site?
- Are there potential costs that we haven't already discussed?
- When is the initial deposit due, and when is the remaining balance to be paid in full?

As with other vital wedding vendors, it's imperative to be highly selective when choosing a florist. In this regard, however, it works to your advantage that the field of florists is so highly competitive. Florists, like few other wedding service providers, are very willing to negotiate prices if it means snagging business away from competing florists, especially if your wedding is not during a peak season. Don't be shy about bringing in quotes from other florists. Let them battle it out to secure your business. Chances are, you have enough bills to pay as it is. Whatever you save on flowers will readily be consumed elsewhere in your wedding budget.

Who's Doing the I Do's?

The selection of a wedding officiant is never to be taken lightly. Their choice of the person who actually will perform the ceremony is arguably the most important joint decision for the bride and groom. Although conventional wisdom dictates that you merely need anyone qualified in the eyes of the law to unite you and your bride in marriage, it really does take the right person to transform an ordinary ceremony into an unforgettable, eloquent celebration of your love for one another.

Because your choice of a wedding officiant is both delicate and important, some argue that selecting the person who will officiate your wedding should be the first decision made in the planning process. Men and women of the cloth are professionals whose services are unendingly courted by couples planning to marry. If your hearts are set on one individual in particular, contact him or her at your earliest possible opportunity to discuss potential wedding dates and begin a consultation process, which can be as helpful as it is spiritually uplifting.

Of course, not every marriage ceremony will be officiated by a religious leader. Civil leaders, perhaps one in your family, are frequently called upon to perform the wedding ceremony. They, too, have busy calendars that quickly fill up during peak wedding seasons. Whoever you choose, this person will unite you and your bride in marriage, so consider the choice carefully.

If you're lucky, either you or your fiancée have a pre-existing relationship with a religious leader or judge. If not, you can't necessarily ask for a recommendation from your caterer or florist. The religious route to marriage can be arranged only by visiting local houses of worship and meeting personally with religious leaders who hopefully will make you feel comfortable and welcome. As always, be certain to discuss availability, building-use policy, whether or not interfaith unions are acceptable (if applicable), and, if either you or your bride has previously been married, if the officiant is allowed to marry a divorced individual. Fortunately, most religious officials will know which questions to ask you, rather than the other way around.

Perhaps most important, try to find a wedding officiant with whom you and your fiancée get along swimmingly. When Christa and I decided on the church to host our wedding and the pastor to preside over the ceremony, it was a decision that started a long-standing relationship with a church that we are now incredibly proud to call "our church." Naturally, such a development not only strengthened our faith, it also strengthened our relationship.

Whether you take the religious route or a civil path, be sure to find someone to preside over your vows that sincerely reflects your personalities and values both as individuals and as a couple.

PLANNING THE HONEYMOON

After planning a wedding, it should come as no surprise that a honeymoon is more than just a vacation on which newlyweds mark the start of their new life together. It is also an escape from the cloud of insanity that has hung over their heads for months.

For more than six months prior to our wedding, my fiancée and I wavered among a host of locations that were as different from one another as you could possibly imagine. Ultimately, the ballooning expenses of our wedding made it particularly difficult for us to decide on an agreeable and affordable honeymoon location, let alone how we were going to pay for it.

Luckily, less than a month prior to our wedding (and I recommend never waiting this late to book a honeymoon), my first book was scheduled for release. Although my book tour would not begin until later that year, I spoke to an old friend about my hopes of visiting Washington, D.C., for the first time in my life while traveling to promote the new book. My friend had spent the last few years working in the White House as a press assistant. Amazingly, he said that if I ever made it out to D.C., he would be able to give Christa and me a personal tour of the west wing of the White House.

After fewer than three minutes of deliberation, Christa and I decided to forget waiting for the book tour and instead immediately book a honeymoon in our nation's capital. By the end of that afternoon, our flight and hotel reservations had been made, and we were preparing for an extensive security background check to gain access to perhaps the most famous residence in the world.

Four days after our wedding, we found ourselves passing through the secret-service checkpoint at the northwest gate of the White House and literally strolling up the lengthy driveway of 1600 Pennsylvania Avenue.

Incredibly, my friend had not only arranged a personal tour, which brought us to the Oval Office, the Cabinet Room, and the Rose Garden, he also managed to secure a spot for us at a small function in the East Room, where the president was in attendance.

Our White House honeymoon was not only one of the most memorable, patriotic, and profoundly inspiring experiences of our lives, it also was a surprisingly romantic and unforgettable vacation that my wife and I continue gush about even today.

One can only imagine, then, how astonished I was to encounter a barrage of people (including some family and friends) who initially derided the idea of a D.C. honeymoon as unromantic and altogether boring. Instead, they would rather have seen Christa and me prepare for a beachside rendezvous in some tropical locale. As with other aspects of our wedding planning, everyone weighed in with opinions about what we should do and where we should go on our honeymoon. And virtually no one thought that a capital getaway would be an enjoyable experience.

In retrospect, our honeymoon exceeded not only our expectations but also those of even our harshest critics. What we gained from the experience was the lesson that honeymoons can stray from convention and should reflect the unique personalities of the bride and groom. If the beach isn't your thing, don't force it. Although you may not have a friend that can get you into the White House, there are many unconventional honeymoon spots that, on the whole, will better suit your style, reduce the strain on your wallet, and create a memorable experience that will last a lifetime.

If you're in charge of booking the honeymoon, keep originality in mind while sifting through potential destinations. Unless the usual suspects have already captured your fancy, stray from anything customary and—with your bride's agreement, of course—prepare for a getaway unlike anything you might previously have imagined.

Whether you bask in tradition or buck convention doesn't really matter, as long as you and your bride are together and happy. Often, booking the honeymoon is the first major decision (and biggest expense) you will make together as a couple. No matter your getaway objectives, the process of planning your romantic vacation should closely follow a series of steps that hopefully will allow your honeymoon to turn out exactly as you hope.

First, establish a budget. Deciding even a ballpark estimate on what you can afford for your honeymoon will most likely eliminate more possible destinations than it will add. Occasionally, couples are encouraged to spend more than they have in anticipation of hefty monetary gifts at the wedding. Now, if you already have substantial pledges to confirm such speculation, then perhaps that's not such a bad idea. Otherwise, play it safe and budget only what you can afford today. If you end up with extra money, there will be no shortage of opportunities to enjoy that loot while you're actually on vacation.

Second, hash out all the elements of excitement and fun you and your fiancée hope to experience on the honeymoon. What sorts of activities sound appealing? What climate would best suit your just-married mood? Make a list of everything you both want as individuals and as a couple. This should also help further narrow your options. Just be sure to not overload your itinerary with things to do. There's a strong probability that you will find an assortment of activities while at your destination that you hadn't previously anticipated.

Finally, take your list of preferences to a travel agent. Despite what you may have heard, there is no added expense and, assuming you haven't already selected your destination, a travel professional can provide you with a smorgasbord of suitable conventional and unconventional travel destinations. He or she then can make all the arrangements without any additional fuss on your part. Just remember to discuss with your agent any special requirements you may need to consider if you're leaving the country. From passports to vaccinations, don't be left in the dark on any pre-honeymoon tasks that you might not have considered.

When you finally reach your destination and begin celebrating in earnest, remember that your honeymoon is a time to enjoy a few days of much needed rest and togetherness before the real world dictates the course of your days until the next vacation. Really slow down to enjoy the experience, photograph everything, and let the occasion serve to bring you and your wife even closer together.

A SUPERSTITIOUS WALK DOWN THE AISLE

On more than one occasion throughout our planning, my fiancée and I couldn't tell the difference between preparing for a wedding and preparing for Halloween. At every turn there was someone pushing off a new superstition on us. From common activities to avoid to unorthodox meals to consume, there was enough talk of good luck and evil spirits to even make a voodoo practitioner roll his eyes.

Shortly before the wedding, my grandmother called to ensure that my fiancée would have "something old, something new, something borrowed, and something blue." Throwing me for a loop, she also added "and a sixpence for your shoe."

At first I thought granny had been hitting the sauce again. But it turned out that the line about a sixpence is the lesser-known fifth "necessity" often excluded from the old, new, borrowed, and blue foursome. Apparently, the sixpence in the shoe symbolizes wealth and a prosperous future.

In the immediate weeks and days preceding your marriage, people you never expected to be superstitious will come out of the woodwork to offer every bit of unwanted counsel you can barely stomach. What's unfortunate, though, is how many couples legitimately freak out in response to these illogical caveats.

Let's face it, there are plenty of couples living long and prosperous lives that didn't come anywhere near a sixpence on their wedding day. The same goes for grooms who saw their brides before the ceremony and couples who endured rain on their big day.

As you will probably observe ad nauseam, some superstitions are quite silly while others are actually very romantic. No matter how seriously or superciliously you approach them, they're impossible to wholly avoid. The important thing to remember is to have fun with the superstitions you either embrace or have forced upon you.

Weddings have become a breeding ground of superstitions because so many strongly believe that what happens on the actual wedding day sets a tone that will last for the entire marriage. So even if a few annoying friends and relatives persistently push their superstitions onto you, keep in mind that they are merely trying to bestow the utmost in good luck upon you and your bride.

Plus, the "good luck milk bath" many superstitious folks recommend can actually be quite exhilarating. At least that's what I've heard. I wouldn't personally know. Really.

CHAPTER 5

THE FINER DETAILS

While you may have been told many times to never sweat the details, when it comes to planning a wedding, don't buy it. Although you may already be well on your way to pulling off a magnificent event, never underestimate how quickly plans can go awry when you fail to consider all the little details of the occasion.

Even though we've already tackled what are traditionally the biggest challenges of the process, you simply cannot afford to allow the smaller aspects to fall under the radar. When it comes to preparing for the big day, nothing can be taken lightly.

No wedding has ever been pulled off without a hitch. From the groom whose cat pooped on his tuxedo the night before the wedding to the bride who had an allergic reaction to her new birth control medication, I have observed many close friends confront a myriad of disasters.

In short, something goes wrong for practically every couple. And most of the time, such dilemmas are born of the so-called minor aspects of the wedding. Although the to-do list presented below may seem surprisingly difficult to screw up, approach every aspect of wedding planning—large or small—as though the entire wedding depends on its outcome.

GIFT REGISTRY

A dreamy notion has certainly entered more than a few marrying minds in wedding seasons past. "Perhaps," you think, "if we don't register for gifts, people will just give us money instead! Doesn't that sound great?"

Don't do it. You don't even want to consider the amount of time you may have to spend returning and exchanging items. The last thing you need is to spend as much time running errands after your wedding as you did before it.

I have yet to encounter a single newlywed couple that, when opting out of the gift registry process, ended up with a nice pile of cash. Instead, they were left with three toaster ovens, two coffeemakers, and a variety of other duplicate gifts that amounted to less money than if they had actually taken the time to register at one lonely store.

For whatever reason, wedding guests like to bring something physical to the party. Many will indeed give money (you hope), but most will also offer a pretty package containing a hand-selected present to hopefully make your new life much easier and happier. And without a gift registry to guide those selections, it's unreal just how ugly the gift-giving process may turn.

If you decide to register, keep three points in mind. First, don't go in unarmed. Before visiting your Bed Bath & Beyond, scour as many catalogues and magazines as you can find. Collect the names and photos of products you're surely going to want as newlyweds. Second, be mindful to stagger the prices of gifts you want across a healthy spectrum. Some guests won't be able to afford the three hundred dollar comforter for your new bed. However, they'll have no problem with the fifty dollar iced tea brewer. Third, always schedule an appointment with someone at the store where you'll be registering. They will offer helpful hints on the process and ensure you don't get too carried away with the gift registry gun.

THE VIDEOGRAPHER

We've all known more than a few newlywed couples who were simply overjoyed to receive their four-hour long wedding video set to cheesy elevator music and featuring the outstanding special effects that defined the music videos of the early 1980s.

Although you probably will want a video recording of your ceremony and reception, I have witnessed far too many couples struggle with the selection of their videographer and, even worse, try to cut corners with other more important vendors in order to get the "best videographer" the yellow pages had to offer.

Without question, many videographers produce stellar work that captures your wedding with the flair and panache of an epic cinematic presentation. And most of the time, such a gifted videographer will charge you as though he really is producing a big-budget Hollywood flick. Now, if you can afford it, there's no harm in having your ceremony commemorated with style. But if money is tight, put as much of your resources as possible into your photographer, and let a family member or friend with a home video camera serve as your videographer instead.

Unlike your wedding photos, which are likely to adorn your humble abode for the rest of your lives together, a wedding video is something you primarily just know is there. Prior to getting married, you may be possessed of the notion that you're going to watch this video on your anniversary for the next fifty years. More realistically, after the initial viewing, the video will rest in storage and gather more dust than it will garner attention.

Ten years ago, the chasm between amateur and professional-grade video quality was undeniably noticeable. However, today's modestly priced digital camcorders are capable of producing broadcast quality sound and video. Many software companies sell incredibly simple computer-based editing programs for less than a hundred dollars. If you have the time or the interest, it might be a romantic experience to edit your wedding video either for or with your wife. Technology has never made a process easier or more affordable.

In my younger days, I worked as a professional videographer and filmed dozens of weddings. What started as a hobby with close family and friends turned into a surprisingly lucrative business driven exclusively by referrals. And although I remain friends with scores of talented videographers, many agree that most couples are probably better off recording their wedding without the assistance of a professional videographer, just as my wife and I ultimately did.

If you prefer to hire a professional, be certain to lay ground rules regarding how "creative" he or she can get with your footage. The last thing you want is a highlight reel set to the theme from *Titanic*. Couples often will request nothing more than the raw footage that's been shot. Not only will this give you an uninterrupted audio and video track, you also will save considerably on the videographer's editing services. Best of all, this gives you the opportunity to have it edited at a later time, either by yourself or through another vendor once funds are available.

As always, only work with a vendor whose work you've seen. If you hire through a company, be sure to see the work of the actual videographer who will be assigned to your wedding. Without personally witnessing the quality of the video and its editing, you will have very little on which to base your confidence.

Luckily, if you have already selected your photographer (which should always be done before choosing a videographer) there's an excellent chance that he or she will have worked with top-notch videographers. Take such referrals seriously and explore their availability.

THE BACHELOR PARTY

When it comes to the celebration of a single man's last night of freedom, there are a number of rowdy ways in which this occasion can be commemorated. If your party planning is left to the best man, there shouldn't be much to do on your part except show up. However, if you and your bride have already discussed limitations for your bachelor party (and if you haven't, now would be a good time to do so), relay those ground rules to whoever is in charge of planning it.

No matter how involved you are in setting the boundaries—if any—for your party, be careful not to make the single biggest error grooms make when indulging in this premarital ritual of raucousness. Whatever you do, don't have your party the night before your wedding.

Although this may seem like common sense, you would be utterly astonished at the number of bachelor parties that take place immediately following the rehearsal dinner the evening before the wedding. Some time ago, a wedding that took place in Patna, India, made headlines exactly for this reason. At the ceremony, the villagers in attendance observed that the incoherent groom had arrived much too drunk to get married. What happened, you ask? The bride married the groom's sober brother instead!

Presumably, many bachelor-party planners believe that taking the groom out for drinks and other disorderly conduct the night before his nuptials is the perfect way to loosen him up for the big day.

Wrong!

The last thing you want is to be tired or hung over on your wedding day. Despite what some believe is the easiest day of the entire process, the wedding itself brings with it a host of responsibilities that will require you to be at your best—not only for your own enjoyment of the occasion, but also for your bride. Don't jeopardize your status as an expert groom by blowing it the night before your wedding.

Ideally, your bachelor party should take place one to two weeks before the wedding. And although you shouldn't be in charge of planning the party yourself, there's nothing wrong with setting the tone or laying some ground rules for your night out with the boys.

For starters, you should be in control of who attends your party. If you're trying to keep things calm, don't let the night get out of hand as a result of spending it with all the wrong people—namely, the guys who will keep you up until 5:00 a.m. playing drinking games at your neighborhood strip club. Granted, if this is your idea of a great bachelor party, let the good times roll! Otherwise, keep a close watch on the guest list to ensure that the night remains about what you want, and not what the boys want.

And although you'll certainly want the element of surprise in your guys' night out, don't feel ashamed to provide your bachelor party planner with a list of places you absolutely don't want to visit. Whether it's out of concern for money or that your bride will be ticked that you visited a strip club, establish the parameters you want followed early on.

If there are no parameters to set, then you don't have much of anything to concern yourself with. Just don't have your bachelor party within hours of your wedding ceremony. Nothing else will undo the progress we've made so far as effectively.

WEDDING DAY TRANSPORTATION

When you take into consideration just how many hundreds of hours and thousands of dollars go into planning a wedding, it makes sense that the pageantry of the big day is most often punctuated by a grand entrance of the bride and groom. Appropriate transportation among the day's locations is essential to facilitate the dramatic arrival we all expect on such an occasion.

The traditional mode of wedding transportation is a black or white limousine, although a surprisingly large number of couples are opting for a horse-drawn carriage if one is available and permitted in their area. There are scores of elaborate arrival schemes that can be hatched. But leaving it to the groom to drive the bride in his Celica is not one of them.

Unfortunately, many couples fail to think about transportation until the wedding day itself. If you're planning a small wedding with a limited budget and little professional assistance, you'll likely be occupied with a host of other responsibilities that arguably are more important than transportation. Still, this is a key aspect of the day's festivities and should not be taken lightly or delayed until the last weeks of preparation.

Like other vendors, stylish rental vehicles are hot commodities, especially during peak wedding seasons. And since many weddings compete with prom season for limousine rentals, it's best to make your transportation decisions as early as possible.

At this point in the planning process, your bride is likely to be concerned with the more intricate and finer points of planning. It makes sense for you to take the lead on transportation—a "guy thing"—while she designs the programs, customizes invitations, and invests herself in everything else that requires her highly trained feminine eye. But, as always, be certain to inform your fiancée of the transportation options you're weighing.

When contacting vehicle vendors, ask the same questions you would of any other professional service provider. Discuss fees, how they are determined, and if gratuity is included. For example, the limo provider I initially contacted for our wedding offered additional discounts for multiple events (bachelor party, wedding shower, etc.). See if that's the case and if so, discuss with your bride any other occasion leading up to the wedding that may be appropriate for riding in style.

If you have separated yourself from tradition throughout much of the planning process, transportation should be no different. There is no shortage of clever ways to get from point A to point B. From Harley Davidson motorcycles to an open-roofed double-decker bus, keep in mind that many vehicle vendors offer more than just limos or upscale town cars. From vintage rides to luxury sports cars, you're definitely not limited in choices by any stretch of the imagination.

As an educated groom, you're probably remembering at all times that your wedding is an opportunity for your bride to live out fantasies that have likely been cherished since childhood. When selecting transportation, be mindful of the romantic visions she would be sure to love. Create a memorable ride for her above all else. If that means skimping out on the Maserati that you'd look great in for the sake of a tender carriage ride reminiscent of Cinderella, you know exactly what you have to do.

With enough time and creativity, any situation and any budget can be accommodated to create a memorable journey, no matter how short the ride will be.

Formal Wear

Of all the legitimate complaints a betrothed woman can make about how much more difficult it is for a bride to prepare for a wedding than for a groom, one is more accurate than all the others. When it comes to formal wear, guys really have it made.

For brides, countless visits to bridal shops are required, searching for the gown that suits the bride's figure, presents her favorably, and possesses that intangible quality that makes a wedding gown uniquely her own. Especially given that it is followed by a myriad of fittings and alternations, the quest to secure the ideal wedding dress is an elaborate, exhaustive, and expensive process.

The groom, on the other hand, can be fitted once for a standard rental tuxedo (and in about an hour) at a cost of roughly one hundred and fifty bucks, or sometimes even cheaper. And unlike the bridesmaids, who often have their share of ordeals with their wedding attire, the groomsmen largely have it just as easy as the groom.

When it comes to formal wear, under no circumstances do you have the right to complain, especially to your fiancée. Should you do so, such complaints will likely be met with a thunderous tirade justly putting you in your place.

Although men have very little to concern themselves with in terms of wedding apparel, they are certainly not excused from putting adequate thought into the selection process. Do you prefer, for example, a double-breasted tuxedo jacket, or is a tailcoat more appropriate for your wedding? How about your choice of collar? Will a wing collar be a good look for you, or is a crossover collar more your style? These are all important questions that a savvy groom will ask, not only to ensure that he looks his best, but also to try to balance the effort his fiancée will be making to make herself a vision of beauty.

In keeping with the expert opinions at www.jimsformal wear.com, the official Web site of one of America's foremost formal-wear providers, not all tuxedos are alike. The effect of even small differences in jackets and collars can be "flattering or fatal," depending on your unique look and body type.

According to Jim's Formal Wear,

> Short and slender gentlemen should look for single breasted jackets with long lines (which elongate the body). Selection of the right pant style is key, too. Double pleated trousers are a good choice

for gentlemen with short, slender frames. And the perfect pant leg should always break slightly on top of the shoe and angle a bit downward in back. This body type can wear vests and ties in colors and patterns.

Short and stocky gentlemen with athletic or muscular body types look best in tuxedo jackets with slim collars. The top button should fall at the small of the waist to give the torso a leaner look. Pants should extend as low as possible on the foot, angled slightly in the back to elongate the leg. Be sure to avoid too much of a break on the foot, otherwise the pant will look sloppy. Choose colorful vests and ties carefully.

Tall and husky gentlemen with broad shoulders and muscular frames look best in shawl collar tuxedos. Jacket length is especially important. To determine a good fit, we suggest that the gentleman place his arms at his sides and relax his hands and fingers. His fingertips should touch the bottom of the jacket and his shirtsleeves should extend one-quarter to one-half inch beyond the jacket sleeve. The fit of the jacket may need to be just a bit loose to provide ease of movement. Also, gentlemen with thick necks and wide faces should avoid narrow ties and wing tip collared shirts that look constrictive. Instead, opt for a laydown collar shirt and bow ties. Choose colorful vests and ties carefully.

Tall and slim gentlemen look well in just about every tuxedo style! Jacket buttons closed up high on the waistline look especially good, and a high shoulder line is better than a natural one. Garments should be full, while still following the lines of the body, and trousers should have a higher rise with more of a break in the pant. This body type can easily wear vests and ties in colors and patterns.

–Courtesy of jimsformalwear.com

No matter how the experts weigh in, you deserve to be happy with your selection of wedding attire. As part of your journey from novice groom to expert groomologist, one of the key steps is learning patience—with your bride, with others, and, especially, with yourself. Take as much time as you need to find the threads that will turn heads. Although you will almost certainly take a back seat to your bride on your wedding day, the guests will see you in your formal wear before they see your bride in her gown. While you briefly have their attention, make it count.

SELECTING YOUR CREW

Before your bride even met you, she probably already knew who would be her maid of honor and who would serve as her supporting cast. Unless her selection process was complicated by having to leave out a sister or a longtime friend for some reason, your bride likely sailed through the nomination process for choosing her bridesmaids. The end result of this endeavor was a number you need to pay attention to. This is the number you now have to match with gentlemen of your own.

No matter whether you need three or ten guys, just be careful your selection isn't based on family or friends demanding to be in the bridal party. Above all else, your best man and groomsmen should be chosen because they are your closest buddies.

When it comes to crowning the best man, you may already know exactly who you're going to choose. If not, you probably have at least a short list of contenders. As you're surely aware, it's important that your best man be among your closest friends, someone who has always stood by you and vice versa.

Think carefully about who you most want at your side on the most important day of your life (besides your lovely bride, of course). Your best man will calm your nerves before the ceremony, lead the pack of groomsmen in their list of delegated duties, and toast you (or roast you) with a personal story at your wedding reception. Whoever you know who you can't envision going through your wedding without is your hands-down choice for best man.

A factor that often complicates the choice of individuals who'll stand up at your wedding is logistics. As you've already learned, there is nothing inexpensive about getting married. If your first choice of best man lives three thousand miles away, and neither of you are financially capable of taking on the travel costs, it is appropriate to speak with your best friend about the situation, but not to pressure him (or yourself) to find a way to make it work.

Even though you know your own budget, you may not know the budgets of your buddies. And standing up at weddings can be quite pricey. It's imperative to consider all that is required of your best man and groomsmen before putting them in the awkward position of having to decline the opportunity for financial reasons. The bare bones financial requirements include:

- Renting formal wear and shoes, plus availability for at least one formal-wear fitting
- Travel and accommodations, if necessary
- Other expenses associated with the wedding (bringing a guest, a wedding gift, etc.)

Although I have suggested on many occasions that the bride should be given her way in many parts of the planning process, there's one place where groomology draws a line: you do not need to yield to your bride should she voice unreasonable objections to your heartfelt selection of a best man. If she doesn't like your choice, it is her responsibility to respect your decision and make the most of it, just as you certainly would if the roles were reversed.

Most of the time, when a bride voices concern about her husband-to-be's choices for groomsmen, it is because she is convinced that one of the boys is too uncouth for such an occasion and will make a rowdy mess of the wedding. Fortunately for her, as an expert groom, you understand the need to express to your groomsmen exactly what is expected of them on your wedding—in terms of both their responsibilities and their behavior. If you succeed in corralling your posse's wildness, not only can you have your choice of groomsmen, but you also will earn new respect from your wife.

'Tis Better to Give

As a gesture of gratitude for their time, energy, and affection, it is only right to provide those standing up at your wedding with a small token of appreciation.

Gifts for the groomsmen are traditional, in the sense that grooms have been giving gifts to their groomsmen for ages. Yet, the choice of these gifts is nontraditional in the sense that every batch of groomsmen is different. Accordingly, they deserve gifts to suit their individual personalities. Unless you're lacking all creative thought, you won't find a truly meaningful gift for your guys in a bridal store at the mall.

A few years ago, my best friend from childhood asked that I serve as his best man. The evening before the wedding (which is the appropriate time to give such a gift), he gave me a present that was personalized and every bit as thoughtful as it was appropriate: a new edition of a well-known publisher's guide to help encourage my budding career as an author. Incredibly, it was Mike's gift that helped me down the path to getting this very book published. Talk about a groomsman gift that keeps on giving! Come to think of it, I should have dedicated this book to Mike.

Although convention holds that all your guys receive the same gift, groomology recognizes individuality in all aspects of the matrimonial process. If you have the time, foresight, and creativity, reward each man who stands up for your wedding with a personal token of your affection that speaks directly to your relationship with that individual. It doesn't have to be elaborate or expensive. It can even be homemade. Just make sure that it touches the recipient in a serious or humorous but undoubtedly poignant way.

There's no need to purchase individual groomsmen gifts if that's not your thing, however. For example, a modern gift often will offer an opportunity to gather again in the near future—tickets to a ball game, a gift certificate to a popular old hangout, or just an IOU for a barbeque in your backyard after the honeymoon. Keeping your relationship tight with your closest buddies can be difficult after marriage. But by making this effort early on, you're doing your best to preserve the relationships that will be beautifully showcased as you all share the altar on what will hopefully be the happiest day of your life.

LICENSE TO WED

It might be the most important license you will ever obtain. But once the religious or civil leader that marries you signs it, its functionality is actually limited to legal considerations that arise mostly after your wedding. For example, your wife will need a copy of your marriage license to legally change her name and Social Security number. With only a few other potential uses, your marriage license can stay safely tucked away with other valuable papers that you need maybe once every twenty-five years.

Nonetheless, your marriage simply won't be recognized by law without a marriage license signed by the authorized person who performs that marriage ceremony. It should come as no surprise, then, why it's a big deal when the groom forgets to bring the marriage license to the wedding for a signature.

Although every state is different in terms of the waiting period once you apply for a marriage license, you usually will be able to obtain it within one week, if not much sooner. More confusingly, however, are the license expiration dates. That is, if you obtain a marriage license too long before your wedding, it may expire by the time you actually get married. Most states require a wedding license to be obtained no more than thirty or sixty days prior to the wedding and returned immediately after it's signed by the individual officiating your ceremony. Once on file, your marriage license acts as the government's official record of your marriage.

In most states you can apply for a marriage license at your county clerk's office.

A few minutes of research online should provide a wealth of information about your state's marriage license application process. No matter where you apply, both you and your fiancée will need to be present and provide as much identification as possible (driver's license, birth certificate, passport, etc.). Once the application is completed (usually for a small fee), you'll need to discuss and determine whose responsibility it is (yours or hers) to maintain possession of the license until the wedding.

When you make your premarital checklist of chores in the days leading up to the wedding, scrawl a note in neon red across the top of the page, if necessary, to remind yourself to bring the license to the ceremony. (Then again, a savvy groom would think outside the box and ask his best man to remind him to bring the marriage license. Redundancy is a foolproof mechanism to ensure that the groom never drops the ball.)

THE "WHAT'S NEXT" GAME

Despite the unrelenting double-checked to-do lists that cluttered our living space for months before the wedding, Christa and I, incredibly, still found ourselves dumbfounded on more than one occasion during our reception when confronted with something we had somehow still forgotten to anticipate.

Looking back, our biggest mistake was failing to play the "What's Next" game.

When it comes to pulling off a wedding, transitions are among the trickiest aspects of the entire occasion. With so much to do and such tight time frames in which to do them, one minor setback or ill-prepared activity can throw a wrench into a smooth flowing operation and quickly turn your party from swinging to sluggish.

I'll never forget the look on my beaming bride's face when, shortly after we were introduced and seated for dinner, our sweet reception hall coordinator, Wendy, patiently asked who would need the microphone to offer a prayer before the meal. Frustrated by our own poor-planning, Christa and I, who are surprisingly more religious than you would expect from two people who forgot about the dinner prayer at their own wedding, thought on our feet and decided that Christa would continue to think on her feet and wing the prayer altogether.

Thankfully, my better half pulled it off. And, although it is most unorthodox for the bride to deliver the prayer before dinner, we made the most of our embarrassing situation without panicking, or even worse, showing our guests that we goofed. Ultimately, however, this example stresses the need to do more than just accumulate a list of big and small responsibilities, tasks, and objectives. As we learned the hard way, the transitions to and from one part of the wedding to the next warrant just as much attention as the major spotlight activities (dinner, cake cutting, the first dance, etc).

What Christa and I should have done is play the "What's Next" game. That is, we should have documented every chronological segment of our wedding and reception on paper while taking note of the easy-to-forget transitions that are required for moving from one important activity to the next. Naturally, we anticipated dinner following the introductions. But without a wedding planner and much outside assistance, Christa and I were overwhelmed with so many planning burdens that forgetting the prayer between introductions and dinner was much easier to do than one might otherwise expect.

By sitting down with your bride to examine all anticipated transitions throughout your wedding and reception, you are taking a great stride toward making your big night run like a well-rehearsed Broadway production.

INDEPENDENT STUDY

Do you have any idea how long, boring, and utterly impractical this book would be if it covered in great detail every aspect of a wedding ceremony's preparatory stages? From teaching you how to prepare invitations in calligraphy to offering step-by-step instructions for tying a perfectly knotted bow tie, there is virtually no end to what *Groomology* could possibly cover.

I'm presenting only the most important and vital wedding planning advice to achieve the best outcome: reduce stress for the bride, facilitate a smooth ceremony, and optimize enjoyment for all.

NEED A CHEAT SHEET? CHECK OUT THESE MUST VISIT WEBSITES:

GroomGroove.com

Groom411.com

Groomsonline.com

Thegroomguide.com

Although we have covered a great deal of material pertinent to our objectives, now that the major and minor planning issues have been discussed from the proactive groom's perspective, it is time for you—possibly with your bride—to take inventory of all that has been accomplished, all that has been learned, and all that is yet to be done.

Four Common Groom Gaffes to Avoid

No matter how in-touch or on-top-of-things you think you are, there are common mistakes made by almost every groom that should always be kept in mind:

1. Don't Pretend Amateurs Are Professionals.

On many occasions throughout my life, I have been asked by friends (looking to save a buck, of course) to help plan events, seminars, and other functions simply to avoid hiring a professional to do the same. When it comes to wedding planning, there's nothing wrong with a lot of help from family and friends. In fact, we all need it. The only real problems begin when we expect professional results from amateur assistants. In other words, don't ask your sister who once made an edible fruit cake to prepare your ornate wedding cake for two hundred people. Of course, this sounds only logical, yet there is never a shortage of couples who have to confront the consequences of putting too many professional responsibilities into the hands of amateur players.

2. Get the Stamp of Approval

Every year the post office returns thousands of wedding invitations for insufficient postage. Much of the time a regular postage stamp won't cut it. In fact, the majority of modern invitations require upwards of sixty cents. Save time and money the first time. If your beaming bride turns over her beautiful handmade invitations to you for delivery arrangements, weigh one of the invitations at the post office and apply the required postage to each. The post office has little remorse for marrying couples that get this wrong. And brides-to-be have even less remorse for grooms responsible for the mishap.

3. Don't Botch the Marriage License

Marriage licenses can be surprisingly complex and easy to bungle. The rules surrounding this seemingly simple piece of paper can actually prove quite bothersome. For example, if you aren't mindful of your state's laws regarding how long a marriage license is valid, you may be prohibited from legally tying the knot on your wedding day. In some states, a wedding license is only valid for thirty days prior to the wedding. If you're unaware of this time line and you obtain a license thirty-one days before your wedding, you're out of luck.

4. No Crash Diets

There remains a lingering myth about the unhealthy extent to which some brides go to shed a few extra pounds before their wedding day. It is rarely acknowledged, however, just how many grooms do the same—and, often, to a much more detrimental result. Dangerous crash diets should be avoided at all costs for either member of the marrying party. The temptation to look one's best is always prevalent before a wedding. Just don't let yourself run the risk of serious illness or permanent damage because of it. Every year, countless men and women get sick, fall behind schedule, and seriously harm themselves trying to drop a lot of weight in little amount of time.

CHAPTER 6

THE OTHER
TO-DO LIST

Confronted with forthcoming deadlines, floral dilemmas, and family drama, two months before our wedding, my fiancée was an emotional wreck.

Despite my involved presence, a clear line remained between what was my turf and what was hers. And, regrettably, for a time there was little I could do directly to mitigate the predicaments that my bride faced on an ongoing basis.

So, with few other options within my reach, I did what any decent groom in my position should do. I purchased an illegal gift for my fiancée.

At that time, it was unlawful in the United States to sell or purchase from a domestic distributor the alcoholic beverage known as absinthe—a mildly hallucinogenic European brew that Vincent Van Gogh famously consumed before cutting off his earlobe.

Luckily, according to a fuzzy, dated law, it was perfectly legal to purchase absinthe from overseas and have it shipped to the States.

After several weeks of research to ensure that my purchase would be legal and not provoke the feds to crash through my living room window with guns drawn, I placed my order for one bottle of fine French absinthe for a sum total of just under two hundred dollars.

By now, you're probably wondering how my quasilegal purchase has anything to do with wedding planning. Actually, it has nothing to do with it. And that's the important point—one I can't possibly emphasize enough.

Taking the stress off your bride routinely involves taking your bride's mind off the wedding. A successful groom does more than just engage himself in the planning process. At times, it's also about disengaging the bride and allowing her to recharge her batteries and refresh her besieged brain.

A year before our wedding, my fiancée saw the film *Moulin Rouge*. Although this flick wasn't exactly my cup of tea, Christa loved it and watched the DVD religiously.

One of her favorite scenes depicted Kylie Minogue as The Green Fairy giving Ewan McGregor his first glass of absinthe. Thanks to *Moulin Rouge*, Christa's fascination with absinthe had begun. Needless to say, you can understand her disappointment to learn that absinthe was not legally sold in the United States—a lesson learned at the local bar when Christa attempted to order a shot of it.

Still, with *Moulin Rouge* being one of the few comforting distractions in her life during the planning stages of our wedding, I decided to surprise Christa during a particularly stressful weekend with a bottle of the forbidden brew. And, just as I had hoped, this unexpected gift immediately lightened her mood, took her thoughts off that nagging to-do list, and allowed us to share a moment that reminded us both that the stress of planning a wedding is ultimately worth it.

SWEET ESCAPES

The one thing your fiancée likely needs most right now is the one thing she almost certainly doesn't have time for—a vacation. Luckily, you have the ability to provide a much needed sense of escape whenever you so choose. Best of all, you can pull it off without great expense or even a large time commitment.

The best ideas for surprising your bride with sweetness come from carefully thinking about what she might uniquely enjoy. After all, it's unlikely I would have gotten the absinthe idea from anything off the shelves of my local bookstore.

If nothing more, consider the following list of sweet gestures a source of inspiration. If nothing comes to you when you're trying to think of ways to cheer her up, try one or all of the following. It really doesn't matter which you choose, as long as you regularly and successfully help your bride relax. Show her how much you care with charming gestures that make her forget about the wedding and remember why she fell in love with you.

1. Make a DVD

Few things are as romantic, sentimental, and lasting as a thoughtful collage of photos softly fading into one another while "your song" provides the soundtrack. In the past, producing such a DVD was practically impossible, both for technical and financial reasons. Today you can purchase or download free of charge the software needed to pull off this enormously thoughtful project.

2. Make a CD

Similar to the DVD idea but much simpler to create is a CD that you personally DJ. With the soundtrack to your relationship as the album, record a personal introduction and/or dedication for each song. Make it serious, but funny. Really mix it up. Burn it, and then slip it into her car's CD player when she's not around.

3. Use Photoshop

If you have the Adobe Photoshop software, make your fiancée a photo card that she'll want to frame. If her favorite movie is *Titanic*, paste your head over Leonardo's and tell her she makes you feel like "the king of the world." Always remember, the cheesier the funnier.

4. Create "love coupons"

You know those booklets of "romantic coupons" redeemable for free back rubs, foot massages, et cetera? Make your own! Make them particularly relevant to your fiancée's situation at the time you give her this considerate gift.

5. Play a game

Visit your local novelty shop (naughty or nice) and buy one of the many games currently marketed to couples (engaged or already married). Most are a real hoot and will lead to hours of fun. This makes a great surprise.

6. Write a poem

Old-fashioned? Yes. Still effective? Definitely. Nothing screams romance like a personal poem, the perfect token of one's affection.

RANDOM ROMANCE FACT

More than ten thousand marriages each year are the result of romances begun during work-related coffee breaks.

---

7. Pamper her

Give your fiancée a gift certificate for a professional massage, an afternoon at a spa, a manicure, pedicure, facial, or a visit to the nail salon. There are some things you can't do for her yourself. Luckily, there are people who can.

8. Look to the stars

Read her horoscope in the local newspaper or her favorite magazine. Plan an evening of fun activities around the general theme predicted in the reading.

9. Write a Top-Ten List

Dress up like David Letterman and videotape yourself reading a personalized "top-ten list" of reasons why your fiancée should still go through with the wedding. Show her the video or email it to her.

10. *Bury a time capsule*

Fill a small container with memorabilia, love letters, or any particularly sentimental items. Give her the time capsule and decide where you want to bury it together. Make a simple map of its burial location, store the map for safekeeping, and then determine a point in the future when you would like to unearth it.

11. *Start a journal*

Every night before you go to sleep, write a brief log of your day, or thoughts as they pertain to your upcoming wedding. At the rehearsal dinner the night before the ceremony, give her the journal to read. If you follow tradition and spend the evening apart, you can still be with her as she reflects on your writing.

12. *Disguise a letter*

Send your fiancée a letter at work or at home. You can camouflage it in a regular business envelope. Do it up to seem really serious at first, but then become silly or gushingly romantic. It will brighten her day more than you might expect.

13. *Strike a pose*

Many couples complain that not enough photos were taken of them during their engagement period. You're bound to have plenty from your wedding day, but the months beforehand tend to get lost in the shuffle. Spend an afternoon or evening taking digital photos together or of one another. Go out to dinner, to the park, the mall—anywhere for a change of scenery—and have your own personal photo shoot.

14. Infiltrate her reading

Replace the bookmark in whatever she's currently reading with a love note. In it, tell her to give you a call, and then listen to whatever is on her mind.

15. Send an E-card

Free animated greeting cards can be really adorable and especially touching. Send one for no reason.

16. Plant notes

When she's not around, place a half-dozen gushing love notes in the places around her house or apartment where she's sure to find them quickly.

17. Make plans for her

You're not the only one who can take her mind off the wedding and its stresses. Call a few of your bride's girl-friends and arrange a surprise party for no particular reason, at your place, her place, or even just a local coffee shop.

18. Cook dinner

It certainly isn't new, but preparing a home-cooked can-dlelit dinner is an all-time classic on any list of romantic things to do.

RANDOM ROMANCE FACT

According to the Guinness Book of World Records, *the longest kiss documented lasted an astounding 417 hours.*

19. Broadcast your love

Call your bride's favorite radio station and dedicate a song to her while she's driving to work or while you're at home together.

20. Go Retro

Forget all the latest bells and whistles—sometimes there's nothing quite as fun as playing old-school Nintendo or her favorite games from the past.

21. Walk it off

Stress relief through spending time together doesn't have to be elaborate or expensive. Taking a nice walk at sunset, sunrise, or even late at night is an incredibly romantic experience.

22. Inflate your thoughtfulness

Pick up a helium balloon that sports a sweet or silly message, and then tie it to her house door or the windshield wiper of her car.

23. Inspire her imagination

Slip a fifty dollar bill inside of a lingerie-store ad or catalog. Leave a note encouraging her to pick up something that you can both enjoy.

24. Crown your princess

The best reason to give your fiancée an "award" is a creative reason. Coronate your bride the winner of a romantic title or silly honor that you've thought up, and have a plaque engraved to commemorate the achievement.

25. Send a steamy message

When your bride is in the shower, write a romantic message on the steamed mirror.

26. Bring home the spa

It takes little more than a few candles, mood music, and essential bath oils to create an at-home spa environment that is sure to soothe and relax.

27. Romance her, one piece at a time

Take a pair of scissors to a brochure for a fancy restaurant or weekend getaway venue (somewhere you actually plan on taking her). Mail her one piece of this romantic jigsaw puzzle at a time, and see how long it takes for her to figure out where you're taking her.

28. Plant a tree together

Find a local spot where it is permissible to plant a tree. Go for a walk one evening and plant a tree together. Return often to watch it grow. Plan to carve your names in it one day. This will forever be "your tree" and a romantic place to visit for a picnic, outdoor nap, or stargazing.

> ## RANDOM ROMANCE FACT
> *Husbands who kiss their wives before going to work are believed to live five years longer than those who pass on the morning good-bye kiss.*

29. Make a romance calendar

A great way to keep romance alive is to schedule it! Maintain a special calendar (preferably one made with photos) earmarking dates to remember and special things to do together. It can be a source of romantic inspiration and excitement.

30. Write her a love prescription

Print from your computer a mock prescription sheet, and handwrite a romantic therapeutic activity of your choosing. Make sure the patient follows doctor's orders.

31. Heat things up

Whether it's at a fireplace inside or a bonfire outside, arrange an evening with your loved one in front of a fire.

32. Sing to her

What could be sweeter—or funnier—than a song written just for her and sung by you? Talent not required.

33. Check the news

Check your local newspaper or community guide to find an interesting event that you and your fiancée wouldn't ordinarily attend. Get out and spice things up by doing something new.

> ## RANDOM ROMANCE FACT
> *Only 14 percent of brides are engaged for more than one year prior to the wedding.*

34. Drink up
Take your bride to a nearby winery. Savor the experience, and be sure to bring back a bottle to enjoy at a later time and reflect on your romantic excursion.

35. Arrange tea for two
If tea is a favorite brew for your bride, make a gift basket filled with an assortment of teas and coffees to achieve different moods and celebrate individual moments.

36. Trust the DVD
The local video store, Netflix, and On Demand remain great places to find romance. Although any film geared toward a female audience is likely to be appreciated, there's nothing like a comedy to release stress and inspire an enjoyable evening.

37. Write on the wall
Pick up glow-in-the-dark (erasable, of course) chalk and write a sweet or funny message on her bedroom ceiling.

38. Save the chalk
If possible, use the same writing utensil to leave a message on her driveway for her to see before she departs for or arrives home from work.

39. Take it off
If you and your fiancée are feeling particularly adventurous, invite her to play strip poker. There's no telling where the fun may lead!

40. Offer a warm gesture
The next time she hops in the shower, pamper her by warming the bath towels in the dryer until they're nice and toasty. This makes for a most pleasant surprise.

41. Relocate the romance
Prior to a bath or shower, move candles or heating oils into the bathroom to give her bathing experience a little something extra.

42. Take a swing
It may seem juvenile, but a round of miniature golf can be fun for kids and grown-ups alike. For couples, mini-golf can prove a surprisingly romantic activity when played shortly before sunset on a warm evening.

43. Pop a pill
Purchase a package of her favorite mints or hard candy. Pretend they are now "love pills." Label a faux prescription bottle with the "effects" caused by taking the pills, and recommend a dosage for your bride.

44. Take the show on the road
If staying home to watch TV isn't your thing and the local movie theater doesn't sound like fun, try a good old-fashioned drive-in theater. Although they aren't easy to find,

plenty of drive-ins still exist. They're a ton of fun and can be incredibly romantic.

> ### RANDOM ROMANCE FACT
> *Wild cabbage is often recommended as a particularly potent aphrodisiac.*

45. Go on a blind date
Instead of just going to a new restaurant for dinner, spice up the journey by blindfolding your bride, and let her guess where you're taking her during the trip. Make reservations and call ahead so that you can have champagne at your table upon arrival.

46. Go back to the beginning
If possible, take a trip to the place where you first met. Talk, share a picnic, or just go for a walk and reflect on where you were then and how far you've come.

47. Leave a random "I love you" voice mail message
It doesn't take much to bring a smile to your lover's lips. In most cases, a sincere voice mail while she's at work away from her phone will be a welcome and much appreciated surprise.

48. Take a coffee break
On whim, go to the local coffee shop and spend time together over coffee, tea, or hot chocolate.

49. Serve breakfast

If breakfast in bed isn't a great way to start the day, I don't know what is.

50. Throw a fondue fest

There's nothing wrong with a box of chocolates, but it's far sexier to bring home a basket of fresh fruit and have a chocolate fondue fest for two. Be sure to get cooking oil for melting the chocolate and toothpicks for the fruit.

51. Surprise her with a special place mat

Make a creative dinner place mat full of love notes, silly drawings, and photos. Visit a local diner shortly before you take your fiancée there for lunch. Arrange with a server to have your special place mat on the table at which you'll be seated.

52. Leave town

If schedules or budgets allow, take a short trip to a nearby destination or resort. It'll recharge your bride's batteries and rekindle your romance.

53. Enjoy a sunset

Keeping it simple but romantic, go somewhere where you both can enjoy a quiet sunset.

54. Rub away the stress

Very few women would not appreciate a nice foot, neck, or back rub. Offer them frequently without having to be asked.

55. Pick up the tab

No matter how small it is, pay for one of her routine expenses (cell phone bill, gas for her car, etc.), and don't let her know you did it. Half the fun is letting her discover your thoughtful gesture.

56. Make loads of fun

It's a dirty job, but somebody's got to do it. Not every girl will appreciate the gesture, but if you think yours would, lend a hand around her place and do her laundry as a thoughtful surprise.

57. Seduce her nose

Few things are as relaxing—and ideal for gift giving—as candles. Purchase or prepare an assortment of scented mood candles, and arrange a romantic basket full of your selections.

58. Pass her a note

Slip a romantic love note in your fiancée's jacket or pants pocket when she isn't paying attention.

59. Read to her

Whether it's a book she's currently reading or a story that you've prepared just for her (maybe in your journal), find time to cuddle up in a cozy nook and read to your bride.

60. Draw her a bath

When she least expects it, fill the tub with warm water and her favorite bubble bath. Adorn the room with lit candles. Take her by the hand and show her the relaxing wonderland you've created just for her.

61. Draw her a picture

Childish? Maybe. Adorable? Definitely. If the written word isn't your strong suit, nothing is cuter, funnier, and potentially more meaningful than a work of art born of your own hand.

62. Hit the road

Take a long drive with no particular destination in mind. Stop at a new restaurant or coffee shop and spend time truly listening to one another.

63. Create a holiday

Make up a unique holiday (one in her honor, of course), mark in on her calendar, and celebrate it accordingly.

64. Work it out

A fun idea for couples is to exercise together, either at the local gym or even at home. Anything that gets the heart pumping and the sweat flowing is a good stress reducer, and makes a surprisingly good date.

RANDOM ROMANCE FACT

The term "honeymoon" was originally coined in the early sixteenth century. The "honey" was supposedly related to the sweetness of marriage, and the "moon" alludes to the notion that love in a new marriage, like a harvest moon, will soon disappear.

65. Make it

Even if arts and crafts didn't capture your attention as a youngster, you might want to give it another try with your bride. Tackling a creative project on a small scale can be a fun, memorable experience.

66. Show some skin

Get a fake rub-off tattoo that says something funny (or naughty) about your fiancée. Be discreet and let her discover your tattoo without any guidance.

67. Unleash the animals

Randomly visit a local pet store and play with any particular animals she may like. A guaranteed good time for all.

68. Plan an overnight rendezvous

Book a nice suite at a local hotel for a spontaneous one-night getaway. Use the Jacuzzi, savor the room service, and enjoy some quality time together.

69. Publish your love
Write a story or short novel (for your bride's eyes only) about how you both met and fell in love. If the sentimental kind, she's bound to love it and cherish it throughout your life together.

70. Go camping
Pick a spot, pitch a tent, and plan a romantic evening alone beneath the stars.

71. Speak a thousand words
Without her knowing, change her desktop image to a sweet or silly picture of you that communicates your love for her. Be creative!

72. Feed her
Remember *9½ Weeks*? Recreate it.

73. Get nostalgic
One evening after dinner, bring out old photo albums, poems, videos, et cetera. Reviewing anything that rejuvenates pleasant memories and inspires positive hopes for the future should remain a high priority throughout the planning stages.

74. Go back to school
With only a minimal time commitment and a small financial investment, you and your bride can enroll in some kind of evening class. From martial arts to pottery, there are plenty of interests that may be taken up as a couple.

75. Belt one out

Take your bride to a local club or bar on karaoke night, grab the mike, and dedicate a song to the woman with whom you plan to share your life.

76. Horse around

Start a pillow fight, or encourage any other physical game that will release tension and provide a few fleeting moments of childish fun.

77. Share the Internet

A great way to pass time is to complete a fun online quiz (preferably one not related to weddings) or decorate each other's Myspace pages.

78. Download your devotion

Create a simple Web site about your fiancée and how much you love her. Send the link to her and all her friends. Watch the fun, loving, sweet comments start to fly!

79. Show good lookin' what's cookin'

Look up the recipe for your fiancée's favorite dessert. If possible, make it yourself. Even if it turns out a mess, she'll appreciate the attempt and will have fun telling her girlfriends what you tried to do.

80. Be da man… handyman

Try to fix something of hers that's broken—a toaster, a cabinet, et cetera. It's certainly a sweet gesture, and just about the most practical too.

81. Let the curtain rise

Head for the nearest big city or, if all else fails, your nearest high school to watch a musical or play. Seeing a live stage play together can be quite romantic and very entertaining.

82. Make the news

Place a small ad in the local newspaper expressing your love for the woman of your dreams. Let the day pass and see if it gets back to her. If not, leave the paper out for her to find in the evening.

83. Lend a hand

Help her clean and stay organized and up to speed with her chores. From helping her vacuum to running a simple errand, these mundane deeds are a great help to your overloaded bride.

84. Give her a personalized gift

Whether it's a goofy T-shirt with your picture and a silly message on it or a coffee mug with the same, give her a gift she couldn't possibly find on any retail shelf.

85. Give yourself to her

Offer to be her romantic love slave for a day. Write up a phony certificate authorizing her power over you for a specific period of time. Let her do as she pleases.

86. Be her music man

Give her an iTunes gift card. This will enable her to soothe her moods with the music that she wants—or needs—when she needs it.

87. Wash her wheels

Whether by hand or at the local car wash, give her car a surprise cleaning.

RANDOM ROMANCE FACT

In 1477, the first known diamond engagement ring was given to Mary of Burgundy by Archduke Maximillian of Austria.

---

88. Indulge her sweet tooth

Candy may seem like one of the stalest ideas around, but more women than we may ever know appreciate the gift of fresh, rich, indulgent chocolates.

89. Give her the stars

Write to your fiancée's favorite celebrity at his or her talent agency (easy to find online) to get an autographed photo just for her.

90. Celebrate an unorthodox anniversary

Figure out how many days you've been together. Make her a card acknowledging this unusual anniversary date.

91. Get up in arms

Take a random "cuddle break" whenever possible. Use this brief time to talk, laugh, or just enjoy a quiet moment in one another's arms.

92. Inspire a treasure hunt

Make a map for her to follow to meet you or to find a present.

93. Give a surefire gift

When all else fails, a thoughtful surprise gift certificate to her favorite store (preferably one that will allow her to pamper herself) is never a bad idea.

94. Be old-fashioned

Tradition is popular for a reason. Send her flowers at home or at work. Unless you're a florist or you know your fiancée's favorite flowers, leave it to the professionals to create an upbeat bouquet.

95. Get naked

If skinny-dipping isn't too scandalous for your tastes or hers, give it a try and let the good times (and clothes) fly!

96. Have a drink

If heading out for a few drinks on the town isn't in order, bring home a bottle of her favorite bubbly, and share it in a quiet place where you can both focus on each other and this splendid treat.

97. Call the boss

If your fiancée works and you know her boss is cool, call her supervisor and hatch a scheme where she will be directed to attend a meeting or run an errand at a particular location. Be there when she arrives, and take her out for a quick bite to eat. (This should only be attempted if there's no risk whatsoever for negative repercussions for your fiancée.)

98. Suck it up

Every bride has at least one hobby or interest that her betrothed is not particularly fond of. If only for a limited time, share one of those activities with your fiancée.

99. Give her "groupies"

Create a Myspace or Facebook tribute page or fan group in her honor and invite all of her friends to join. Be sure to leave plenty of sweet or funny messages and sit back and watch as others follow suit.

100. Leave it up to her

Instead of following these or coming up with your own clever ideas, ask her what she would like to do for fun or to escape her stress even if for only a short while. Follow her wishes accordingly and promptly.

FROM SINFUL TO SIMPLE: IDEAS FOR A BACHELOR PARTY… OF A DIFFERENT SORT

If you're not the bar-crawling, stripper-loving, engaged male, your bachelor party can still be a good time for you and your buddies. Here are just few less than conventional options to get your imaginative thoughts flowing.

- *Take It Outside*

  Imagine roughing it in the woods, hanging with your best friends, and drinking as much as you can possibly fit into as many coolers as you can possibly carry. Rather than test your bride's patience with a night of debauchery, test your survival skills with a full day (or weekend) of camping, hiking, rock climbing, fishing, and, of course, sitting around a s'mores fire pit and letting your buds share unforgettable tales about the adventures you've had, the girls you've dated, and all the embarrassing moments that you'd rather forget.

- *A Co-ed Affair*

  If you're planning to do something you would do in front of your fiancée, why not just include her? Believe it or not, the concept of a co-ed bachelor party is gradually becoming more popular. Whether it's a simple gathering at home or an all-nighter on the town, a co-ed bachelor party can be an awesome couples' night of food, games, and whatever else will keep the evening interesting and, most importantly, focused on the groom.

- *Take the Plunge*

  My cousin Jim is not only a recent newlywed, he is also a professional skydiving instructor. He tells me that a substantial chunk of his expansive clientele is composed of men only days (or hours) away from getting hitched. When you think about it, what could be more exhilarating than jumping head first out of an airplane at twelve thousand feet and free falling for over a minute at 120 mph with your closest buddies? It's certainly not for everyone, but your bride will likely prefer you falling from a plane than falling for a stripper.

CHAPTER 7

ONE MONTH BEFORE THE WEDDING

Once you reach the thirty-day window on the wedding, it isn't uncommon for all hell to break loose. With so little time remaining and so much yet to be done, it can seem utterly impossible that everything will come together seamlessly.

A month before our wedding, Christa and I (struggling to balance full-time careers and a long-distance relationship) still hadn't completed a sizable number of tasks on our intimidating to-do list. I had to get fitted for my tux and book our honeymoon, and Christa hadn't finished the centerpieces or prepared the six hours of music needed for our iPod-powered reception.

If you similarly find yourself on the precipice of panic thirty days before your wedding, you're certainly not alone. Besides my own experience with the final countdown to matrimony, I also have yet to encounter a married couple that didn't have a comparable mini crisis during crunch time.

Whether it's fortitude, teamwork, or just plain dumb luck, the overwhelming majority of couples manage to tie up all the loose ends and cruise into their wedding day with check marks all through that once overpowering to-do list. To find peace with planning yourself, remember that the biggest obstacle during the final month of preparation is your own nerves.

Understandably, these last thirty days are significantly more nerve-wracking for the bride than for the groom. For your fiancée, there are final gown fittings, appointments to make, bridesmaid crises to solve, documents to sign, vendors to consult, and her own frazzled wits to manage.

For you, there is commonly a very small list of responsibilities to handle. Apart from making sure your tux fits properly and that your groomsmen have directions to the church, the typical groom merely waits for his bride to direct him to help with other tasks weighing her down.

But as we all know by now, you are definitely not the typical groom. Consequently, you are prepared and equipped to make the final days before the wedding a much more pleasant experience for all parties involved.

RATCHETTING DOWN THE ANXIETY

Routinely, a large portion of the bride's total stress during the final month is attributable to concerns about the many vendors entrusted to facilitate your wedding. Apprehensions about miscommunications, errors, and wedding-day mishaps can cloud a bride's consciousness to a point that she repeatedly checks in with vendors and, as an unintended consequence, actually confuses them in the midst of her own unwarranted panic attack.

Creating a buffer between your bride and your service providers is the first line of defense against a bridal breakdown. By taking charge and letting your fiancée know that you are going to be on top of the vendors like white on rice will do wonders to calm her nerves. At first, she will likely demand personal involvement in the process of confirming details with all the service providers. However, as you move through this process together, let her see how aggressively thorough you are with each vendor. Don't merely put on a show. Legitimately meet with or speak to every hired professional to confirm dates, review plans, coordinate schedules, and walk through the entire day with everyone you have hired to provide a quality service for which there can be no do-over.

After first consulting with your bride, take it upon yourself to:

- Confirm reservations and all plans for the rehearsal dinner.
- Personally contact invited guests who haven't RSVP'd but you believe may still be coming to the wedding.
- Check in with the caterer, and provide him or her with the final guest count.
- Contact the photographer to confirm schedules and discuss the wedding day agenda.

- Speak with your DJ or bandleader to verify plans for the reception.
- Confirm delivery times and locations with the florist and recheck the order.
- If transportation or lodging plans have been made for out-of-town guests, confirm them.
- Check in with the limousine (or other transportation) provider to review services needed.
- Confirm honeymoon arrangements.
- Designate one of your groomsmen as the wedding-day troubleshooter for vendor mishaps.
- Review your budget spreadsheet and prepare for any payments that will be due on your wedding day.
- Check in with your videographer to walk through the wedding day schedule.
- Walk through the ceremony and reception sites again. Determine where you will get dressed, if parking concerns should be considered, if handicapped access is an issue, etc.
- If you have hotel reservations on your wedding night, confirm them. If you still need hotel reservations, make them.
- Meet with or speak to your best man and each groomsman to review exactly what's expected/ needed and answer any questions.

DON'T STEP ON HER SHOES

We've all experienced incidents where our help actually became a hindrance.

The last thing you want is to be an overzealous groom who, despite the best of intentions, disrupts his bride's laserlike focus. This late in the game, your fiancée is bound to be "in the zone." It's all coming down to the wire, and she knows exactly what she needs to do. What she absolutely doesn't need is an eager groom consistently interrupting her train of thought with questions about what you can do to help her. At this point, she won't hesitate to pull you in to carry extra weight. You can see why grooms unlike yourself—that is, those who take a lax approach to wedding planning—find the final month before the wedding extraordinarily difficult: because they aren't accustomed to the process or familiar with the responsibilities. Consequently, an inexperienced groom wandering around trying to get involved during the last weeks of preparation can spell extra stress for both parties and may have severely counterproductive results. Luckily, you will be a seasoned pro by this time and are likely to find the last month one of the easiest—at least for you.

No matter what you do, your bride will probably always be teetering on the brink of a major panic attack in the days immediately preceding the wedding. The way you can help prevent her from actually having one is by closely monitoring exactly what she is stressing about. At times, she will express concern about things over which neither of you have any control. In this case, you have to just let such anxieties run their course. With you close at her side and hopefully implementing many of the strategies and helpful hints previously outlined to ease her mind, your solidarity during these fleeting episodes will help to soothe them.

For the most part, use the last four weeks to stay out of her way, but remain close enough to let her know you're a battle-tested soldier ready to spring into action when drafted. However, this doesn't mean you're going to get to be a slacker during any down time. In the waning days before the wedding, use as much time as you can find for personal chores that only you can perform yourself. It may feel somewhat awkward, but only because you'll be focusing so heavily on yourself for a change. For starters:

- Rehearse your vows (or write them).
- Pick up your marriage license.
- Prepare a groom's survival kit—a bag of emergency items for your wedding day: toothbrush, hair products, a comb, deodorant, mouthwash, sewing kit, Band-Aids, safety pins or straight pins, antacids, electric razor, magazines or CDs/iPod to help you relax, medications you may be taking, and anything else you may want or need in an emergency situation.
- Instead of asking your bride if she still has something to do, (e.g., purchase and bring the cake knife, round up the toasting goblets, select a guest book, etc.), make a to-do list of your own and compare it

with hers. Tackle pressing chores accordingly.

- Hit the ATM, and stuff an envelop with the total amount of cash you intend to shell out for gratuities on the wedding day.
- Arrange to pay bills ahead of time that may come due while you're on vacation.
- Purchase a gift for your bride that you can give her when you separate the night before your wedding.
- Pack for the honeymoon.
- Arrange to have mail and newspapers stopped during your travels.
- Arrange a house-sitter if necessary

Although the last four weeks before the wedding will be particularly stressful, they also will pass very, very quickly. Stay on top of your list, and, more important, stay on top of your bride's mood. Without seeming like an overprotective grandmother, make sure your fiancée is resting well and eating properly. If necessary, employ the techniques discussed in previous chapters—that is, employ some cute or romantic gestures to take her mind off the wedding, even if only for a few minutes.

'Twas the Night Before the Wedding...

Some time ago, a close friend of mine likened his emotions on the night before his wedding to looking through a kaleidoscope.

"You're sort of overwhelmed by all the different things you're seeing and feeling all at once," he said. "At first you don't know what to think, but you just can't help but continue concentrating your eyes forward."

Similarly, the evening of the rehearsal dinner is one that causes both brides and grooms to experience a whirlwind of emotions that run the gamut from fear to exhilaration. At times you may feel so many different things that you don't know how you feel at all. But you keep moving forward because that's all you can do at this point.

Surprisingly, many couples fail to take comfort in the fact that they are rehearsing everything! If there are bugs in the system, the rehearsal provides the ideal opportunity to work them out before the audience arrives and the curtain goes up on a production that you won't soon forget… or, hopefully, repeat.

For you, there are plenty of tasks that remain even in the waning hours before the ceremony. For starters, be sure to give the ring and the clergy fee to your best man at the rehearsal dinner. Traditionally, it is his responsibility to present the ring for your bride during the ceremony and to compensate the officiant after the deed is done. Delegating such responsibilities to a responsible bridal party member means that on your actual wedding day, when your nerves will likely be on end for hours, you won't need to worry about your anxiety making you forget all you need to do. Since there's no way to fully restrain anxiety, focus instead on limiting your to-dos before your I-dos. If, for example, any balances are owed at the reception, once again, entrust a member of the bridal party or a responsible friend to give the checks you've written to the appropriate individuals.

Ideally, you won't wait until the rehearsal dinner to compile a list of things you would like other people to do on your behalf. Such a plan of attack requires foresight, and not just taking a few minutes to scribble a task or two on a cocktail napkin. It would be to your undeniable benefit to make sure that on the rehearsal night, you won't have to worry about doing anything else. Barring any critical planning emergencies that require your attention in the final hours before your wedding, take as much time as you need for yourself. Although this may sound perplexing and utterly contrary to everything you have learned until now, the eve of the ceremony should be used to completely forget about the wedding itself, and to some degree, even your bride. By now, you don't need to maintain that protective sphere over her. The night before the wedding, she will have family and friends to keep her calm, particularly if you are honoring tradition and not spending the night before your wedding together.

Occasionally, the groom will use his dwindling hours of bachelorhood as an opportunity to unwind with a few drinks with his best man and groomsmen. However, just as I warned to avoid at all costs having your bachelor party the night before your wedding, the same applies to drinking one too many at your rehearsal dinner. The prospect of a hangover on your wedding day should be even less attractive to you than seeing David Hasselhoff wearing lingerie. Nonetheless, plenty of grooms can't resist drinking with the guys the night before it all happens. If you drink, be sure to drink in moderation.

It may seem astronomically difficult to find a way to relax organically the night before the wedding, but there are ways that don't involve or encourage substance abuse. Avoid any sleep aids or new medications that could provoke an allergic reaction or leave you groggy or ill by morning. Ultimately, the final night of your bachelorhood requires that you take care of yourself and get as much sleep as possible. And if sleep is still difficult to come by, turn on a flick and just try to chill out.

A cheat sheet for your final night of bachelorhood:

- No wedding is perfect. Should something go wrong, you will deal with it masterfully and not let it spoil the celebration.

- Guests are traveling from near and far to celebrate you and your bride, not to judge the both of you. You will be showered with more love and support than you can anticipate.

- A sense of humor is vital. When confronted with a wedding day mishap, find humor in the incident.

- Unlike the stressful months that have preceded this night, your wedding day will prove a blissful occasion void of stress and filled with joy.

REHEARSAL DINNER FAQS

Q: Where should the rehearsal dinner be held?

A. The rehearsal dinner is usually held at a private home or at a restaurant near the ceremony or reception site.

Q: How formal or informal should the rehearsal dinner be?

A: It's completely up to you. Some couples prefer to barbeque at home while others reserve tables at the most elegant five-star eatery in town. Whether it's a backyard luau or a dressy extravaganza depends on what you want, what is appropriate, and, primarily, what works with your budget.

Q: Who is invited to the rehearsal dinner?

A: Usually, the entire bridal party, the bride and groom's immediate families, the presiding minister, and any other preferred family, friends, and out-of-town guests that have been invited to the wedding.

Q: What's important to remember when planning the rehearsal dinner?

A: There are no rules set in stone. About the only "traditions"— and I use that word lightly—followed are that the best man offers a toast to the bride and groom, the groom toasts his bride and her parents, and the bride then responds with a toast of her own. The rehearsal dinner is also a great time to distribute the attendants' gifts. Otherwise, as long as the rehearsal dinner doesn't lead to a late night, everyone will be warmed up and ready for an enjoyable wedding day.

CHAPTER 8

THE WEDDING DAY

A man sits alone on the couch with his soon-to-be mother-in-law and the family dog. The man is so nervous that his stomach begins to hurt, and he accidentally lets out a little gas. He's horrified until the mother-in-law yells "Rocco!" and the man thinks, She thinks it's the dog! So he lets another one rip, and the mother-in-law yells "Rocco!" again. Feeling confident now, the man lets out a really loud, big, fat one. And she yells, "Rocco! Come here before that pervert craps on you, too!"

As this crude old joke illustrates, there's nothing more effective than a little confidence to soothe a nervous conscience. Then again, too much confidence ultimately can make a bad situation even worse.

When the wedding day finally arrives, you, like millions of grooms before you, may struggle to reconcile your unsteady nerves with your steadfast confidence in your decision to marry. Yet, contrary to the thinking of the ill-advised sideline advisors who urge grooms not to be nervous in the least, the marrying man actually may benefit from a perfectly normal small dose of anxiety. After all, it's always the nervous chaps who make it through their weddings with flying colors. On the other hand, the overconfident, borderline-cocky grooms always seem to end up letting their guards down, making mistakes, and botching wedding-day responsibilities.

After weeks and months of stressful planning, the event you have worked long and hard to help plan is finally here. And it will likely rush by in a whirlwind of activity that will consume your every thought and emotion from the moment you wake up until you go to sleep as a newly married man.

Yes, today is your wedding day—your transformation from groom to husband. Of course, it also represents your promotion from groom to host and greeter. As you can imagine, your wedding day will be one of the most social experiences of your life. And the occasion is rife with opportunities to show others the same charm, patience, and courtesy that you have given your bride throughout this journey. And believe it or not, a little anxiety can go a long way to ensure a stellar performance as the man of the hour.

As many celebrities and entertainers have long emphasized, the butterflies they experience before a major performance can actually serve to enhance the quality of their performance. How? Whether it's attributable to an adrenaline rush or merely to their heightened senses, there's nothing like a little nervousness to truly bring out the best in a person. And when it comes to your wedding day, you can't afford not to be at your best.

AT YOUR BEST WITHOUT REST

Studies have shown that the typical groom sleeps fewer than five hours the night before his wedding. With emotions and anxiety running high, this is an understandable reality. Many grooms find themselves trying to get to sleep while worrying about how well they'll feel the next day if they don't get enough sleep! Still, there's no need to worry about how much sleep you get. Of course, a full night of peaceful sleep is preferable. But in all actuality, no matter how little shut-eye you get, it is unlikely you will wake up with anything less than a healthy bounce in your step and a fire in your belly. A natural euphoria resulting from rushing adrenaline will keep you alert. This is a very helpful fact, especially since the wedding day itinerary is runnin' and gunnin' from start to finish.

But apart from allowing yourself to be a little nervous and accepting the fact that you might not have the best night's sleep, there are a number of additional helpful suggestions that can also be used to assist a groom in preparing for the big day.

WEDDING DAY TIPS FOR THE GROOM

- *Have a hearty breakfast. You're in for a long day. The last thing you want is low blood sugar and a grumpy demeanor to accompany your hectic schedule until dinner is finally served.*
- *Use lots of deodorant.*
- *Keep breath mints with you.*
- *Use your usual razor and shaving cream to avoid razor burn or skin irritation caused by a new product.*
- *Don't drink or smoke before the ceremony, to keep your clothes smelling fresh.*

PUTTING ON THE TUX... AND THE BRAKES.

Having interviewed scores of newly married men about their matrimonial experiences, I found that the majority were astounded by a phenomenon that one man called a "runaway locomotive cut short." For weeks and months prior to the wedding, agendas are tight and schedules are hectic. You never have time to hit the brakes and unwind because you're always accelerating toward more deadlines. And in the end, this inordinately lengthy process leads to a moment that frankly seems to pass all too quickly. After days of too much work and too little sleep, the wedding arrives, and there is virtually nothing to do except enjoy yourself. For many brides and grooms, this realization strikes like a ton of bricks. And, surprisingly, it can seriously inhibit one's ability to let go and savor the occasion. Like setting foot on solid ground for the first few minutes after a ten-hour car ride, it's normal to feel like you're still moving forward. This is precisely how many couples feel on their wedding day.

After speaking with a sizable group of newlywed couples, many confessed that among their only wedding day regrets was not adequately pacing themselves to really enjoy the occasion and absorb the excitement. The wedding day is an opportunity to suspend your managerial mentality and, instead, revel in the fruits of your labor. After all, if you have diligently tended to your responsibilities and wedding-day details and adequately coordinated your vendors and support crew, there is little if anything with which to concern yourself on the wedding day. If anything does go wrong at your ceremony or reception, there's a high probability that only you and your bride will notice. Conversely, if you don't loosen up a bit and try to have a good time, everyone will notice, especially your bride, who may then find it difficult to enjoy the celebration herself.

Ultimately, when the wedding day is finally upon you, it is vitally important that you begin your day exactly as you want it to play out in its entirety: relaxed, at a medium pace, and free of any worries. Luckily, as a savvy, educated groom well aware of the pitfalls that have tripped up less poised grooms, as your day begins, you can relax in the knowledge that you have done absolutely everything in your power to ensure a smooth, successful wedding. The work is behind you. And, hopefully, your bride is happy with all that your teamwork has yielded. At the end of the day, as long as your fiancée is happy and satisfied, you have done your job as a successful groom. The time has now come to celebrate what you, your bride, and your families and friends have worked so hard to orchestrate.

The Day Ahead

On the morning of your wedding day, it is likely that you and your bride will have surprising dissimilar schedules. Because she will probably have more things to do and need longer to dress, her day may start a lot earlier than yours. Nonetheless, it is only your day with which you need to be concerned. Throughout the entire planning stages, you have diligently looked after your bride with unparalleled patience and dedication. Rest assured that on the morning of your wedding day, she is in good hands, capable of getting her through the next few hours until she returns to your loving care once more.

Fortunately, since most wedding ceremonies take place in the afternoon, you have the entire morning to dress to prepare yourself for the day ahead. Unlike your bride, whose day begins in earnest with tons of pre-wedding photos and hours of dress time, you will likely have the luxury of simply getting dressed and driving to the ceremony site.

PRE-CEREMONY CHECKLIST

- *If you've written your own vows, rehearse them a few times, but not excessively.*
- *If your best man has a to-do list, check to ensure he's remembering to follow it.*
- *Bring your groom's survival kit (toothbrush, deodorant, hair products, etc.) to the ceremony site.*
- *Relax and mingle with friends and family.*

When it comes to the wedding ceremony itself, just as no two brides are exactly alike, the same may be said of the diversity of wedding ceremonies. Some last fifteen minutes, while others last two hours. Chances are, yours will fall somewhere in between. And since you've had a rehearsal, there should be no apprehension on your part about how precisely the ceremony will unfold.

Although ceremonies can vary widely, the events that follow the pronouncement of husband and wife rarely change. Like a kitten ready to pounce on a new swat toy, your guests will be ready to pounce as soon as you kiss the bride.

Gathered with your friends and family after the wedding, the reception is where you all come together to celebrate. In this grand culmination of events, the reception is your time to live it up. In the next four to five hours (the length of a typical wedding reception), you will have ample opportunities to do just that. But you won't be doing it alone. You now have a wife.

Throughout much of the day, you will no doubt have your eyes trained on your beautiful bride. Be sure, however, to do more than just share her presence and cherish her splendor. Also make sure that she's okay.

One of the biggest and most common wedding reception mistakes—made by both brides and grooms—is failing to eat. Even though the head table is served first, many couples are too engrossed in mingling that they simply don't get the chance to eat. Avoid this common mistake at all costs. Not only do you deserve to sit quietly and share a memorable meal—one that you personally selected, no less—you also don't want to proceed with the celebration and any alcohol consumption on an empty stomach. Keep in mind that perhaps the only time you and your bride will eat on your wedding day is at the reception. Seize the moment, for your bride's sake and your own.

Apart from the basic activities of taking the time to eat, making the effort to thoroughly mingle, and slowing down to really absorb the splendor of the occasion, there's simply nothing else to do. Unlike every other day preceding the wedding, the evening of your reception presents no rules or challenges. Now it's all about you and your bride. In fact, on your wedding day, there's only one rule to follow: don't leave the reception too early. Chances are, many guests have come from great distances to see you and your wife on this blissful occasion. This will also be a rare opportunity for many of your family members and friends to unite. After all, some families only gather at funerals and weddings. Make the most of it.

Unfortunately, many couples skip out early because they think they should reserve as much energy as possible to, shall we say, have some gas left in the tank once they get to their hotel. Incredibly, however, many couples don't spend their wedding night doing exactly what most of us expect all newlyweds to do. Whether it's attributable to fatigue or out of interest in waiting for the honeymoon, many couples delay the deed for a number of reasons. In this regard, the end of your wedding day should reflect the start. In other words, go with the flow, enjoy yourself, and disregard any expectations that don't mesh with what you and your bride want to do in the moment.

When all is said and done, when you reflect on the process of planning your wedding, you are likely to realize that the lessons learned are more than just guiding principles for being a good groom. In essence, they are also the same principles that make a good husband. The basic rules of groomology—those that call for open communication, unfailing respect, and a constant attentiveness to the emotional well-being of your partner—are the fundamental ingredients of a happy marriage. And may your happy wedding be the start of an unendingly happy marriage.

Groomology Pop Quiz

1. An expert groom is one who:

A. Tackles as much responsibility as he possibly can during planning.

B. Doesn't do much during the planning process except during the final month.

C. Is involved to the desired extent expressed by his bride and required by the unique circumstances of the specific wedding.

2. A contemporary bride can expect to contend with stress from:

A. Trying to live up to the unrealistic expectations being placed upon her.

B. Family and friends who want things done their own way.

C. Attempting to achieve the "perfect wedding" and controlling factors that can't possibly be controlled.

D. All of the above.

3. The majority of marrying females desire a groom who:

A. Will completely stay out of their way.

B. Can handle the bulk of wedding planning.

C. Is sensitive and responsive to their needs and worries.

4. Almost every bride:

A. Takes the planning and preparation of her wedding very seriously.

B. Wants at times to strangle her mother or your mother.

C. Occasionally forgets why she agreed to get married in the first place.

D. All of the above.

5. Which of the following is a rule of groomology:

A. Take time to learn all that is involved in planning and all that is presently wracking her nerves.

B. Understand that every bride is different and expects different levels of involvement from her groom.

C. Be more patient with your bride than you have ever been before.

D. All of the above.

6. The reason so many grooms struggle with trying to understand their bride's seemingly infinite burdens is because:

A. They don't care.

B. Brides intentionally try to be difficult.

C. The betrothed female is engaged in an emotionally volatile process that even she may be struggling to understand.

7. According to our studies, the ideal groom is one who primarily serves as:

A. A subservient minion of the bride.

B. An errand boy with a to-do list.

C. A protector of the bride's emotional sanity.

8. **A significant increase in the number of grooms taking a proactive approach to their weddings is attributable to the fact that:**

   A. Modern men are more comfortable doing girlie things than ever before.

   B. More men than you think actually like wedding planning.

   C. Contemporary couples are marrying later in life, which makes it more likely that grooms will pay for the wedding and want more involvement.

9. **Based on custom, which of the following is primarily considered a groom's responsibility?**

   A. Applying for and obtaining a marriage license.

   B. Selecting formal wear for himself and his groomsmen.

   C. Arranging the honeymoon.

   D. All of the above.

10. **A vital aspect of groomology is reducing stress for the bride. What is the most effective tactic for achieving this objective?**

    A. Reassuring the bride that everything will be all right while never pausing your video game to say so.

    B. Not offering feedback on her problems because you won't have the solutions and you'll probably just make matters worse.

    C. Engaging your bride in pleasant activities and conversation that has nothing to do with the wedding but provides quality and relaxing time together.

11. Many wedding-related planning catastrophes are the direct result of:

A. Not taking seriously the minor planning aspects of the wedding

B. Not making enough decisions with your fiancée.

C. Not spending enough money on the wedding.

12. Brides increasingly require more assistance from their grooms because:

A. Men have innate qualities that best enable them to choose centerpieces.

B. Women don't really have much interest in weddings.

C. The modern bride is a workingwoman far more successful, educated, and self-sufficient than the brides of yesterday. She has less time to prepare a wedding.

13. The first order of business for any groom looking to take a proactive plunge is to:

A. Purchase as many bridal magazines as possible to learn about how weddings are planned.

B. Ask for a to-do list, carry out your responsibilities, and stay out of your fiancée's way.

C. Take his bride by the hand and sincerely ask what her expectations for the wedding really are.

14. Grooms entrusted with substantial planning responsibilities are advised to:

A. Intentionally screw up so she won't ask you to do anything.

B. Visit a variety of vendors and relevant retailers to study the wedding market and prepare for future decisions.

C. Outsource the responsibilities to someone looking for a job.

15. **For grooms just beginning to involve themselves in the planning process, it's important to:**

A. Delay as many decisions as possible until right before the wedding.

B. Take small steps and not be discouraged by common mistakes that are a natural part of the process.

C. Get as much out of the way early on.

16. **For actively involved grooms, it's imperative to:**

A. Take the bride's opinion for granted when making decisions by yourself.

B. Never be embarrassed to ask your bride for input, even when making decisions that were delegated to you

C. Volunteer your wedding for a reality show and not tell your fiancée until the cameras arrive.

17. **Although the groom should have a mind of his own, it's critical to abandon such views if they are eventually:**

A. Proven wrong.

B. Proven inappropriate.

C. Proven to upset your bride past an unacceptable boundary.

D. All of the above.

18. Once the question is popped and the wedding is on, prioritizing all tasks and responsibilities starts with:

A. Setting a budget.

B. Determining the honeymoon location.

C. Selecting the flavor of the wedding cake.

19. A familiar mistake made by couples preparing to marry is:

A. Forgetting to make lists and remain organized.

B. Adhering so rigidly to tradition that the wedding fails to reflect their unique personalities.

C. Neglecting to take time from a hectic planning schedule to cherish one another and reflect on why such stress is ultimately worth it.

D. All of the above.

20. A skilled groom savvy in the art of successful wedding planning knows that:

A. Stress really isn't all that bad for a bride.

B. Weddings are probably easier to plan than some stupid book suggests.

C. It's essential to reduce stress overall, not just absorb it from the bride.

21. When commemorating your last night of freedom with a bachelor party, be certain that:

A. You're home at a reasonable hour.

B. What happens in Vegas stays in Vegas.

C. You don't have your bachelor party the night before your wedding.

22. **To keep the groom looking and feeling his best for the big day, in the last few weeks prior to the wedding, never experiment with:**

    A. A new haircut.

    B. A new medication or food that could cause an allergic reaction.

    C. A new activity that could provoke injury.

    D. All of the above.

23. **Any pre-wedding mishaps should be handled with which of the following:**

    A. Extreme panic.

    B. Urgent attention.

    C. A sense of humor.

24. **One month before the wedding, it's normal to:**

    A. Be nervous.

    B. Have a long list of unfinished tasks.

    C. Fall behind schedule consistently.

    D. All of the above.

25. **What is (are) among the most important points to remember on your wedding day?**

    A. Disregard any expectations that don't mesh with what you and your bride want to do.

    B. Relax, enjoy the day, and remember that the hard part is over.

    C. If anything goes wrong, only you and your bride will likely notice.

    D. All of the above.

Answer Key

1. C
2. D
3. C
4. D
5. D
6. C
7. C
8. C
9. D
10. C
11. A
12. C
13. C
14. B
15. B
16. B
17. D
18. A
19. D
20. C
21. C
22. D
23. C
24. D
25. D

COMMENCEMENT

Congratulations! You, unlike the vast majority of the millions of hapless grooms who marry each year, are now equipped with sacred knowledge possessed by few and envied by many.

As President John F. Kennedy once stated, "For those to whom much is given, much is required." Along with your newly acquired status comes great responsibility indeed. In the days, weeks, and months ahead, you will carry the mantle of an elite class of grooms. You have successfully explored and taken in a wealth of information that will no doubt benefit your bride, and wrestled down the complex aspects of wedding planning that might otherwise have been causes of stress and frustration.

Before, you were simply a novice groom, sweetly expressing interest in taking an active role in organizing your wedding and making the process considerably less traumatic for your fiancée.

Since that time, you have come a along way. The skilled groom expresses legitimate interest and concern in all that matters to his bride; takes over the tasks his bride can't or won't do; is sensitive and responsive to her needs and worries; is mindful of the relationship dynamics of wedding planners; helps his bride resolve both internal as well as external conflicts; gets her to relax with sweet gestures; takes time to learn all that is involved in planning and all that is presently wracking her nerves; understands that every bride is different and expects different levels of involvement from her groom; ungrudgingly accepts the level of involvement his bride expects from him; is thoughtful and creative when it counts... and when it doesn't; and is more patient with his bride than he has ever been before.

I remember well the great uncertainty I felt when I was in your shoes, deciding to become an active, modern groom myself. You may be justifiably nervous about leaving the safe, comfortable state of groom inactivity that has defined generations of grooms before us. The mere thought of hurling yourself headlong into the brutal, harsh world of wedding planning as an involved participant is not, I will admit, a comforting concept to embrace. But I hope your groomology experience has been a gift that will see you through the turbulent, bride-infested waters ahead.

Given the triumphant feat achieved here, the ultimate question now is, to what extent will this alter the default programming that casts most grooms as uninvolved and disinterested until the actual ceremony arrives? The answer is: it's up to you. Whether your training makes a significant impact or a minimal one during the journey ahead depends entirely on how you apply your preparation to the unique circumstances surrounding your wedding. But groomology has taught you that being an expert groom isn't about how much or how little you do. It's about being receptive to your bride and her apprehensions, and knowing what things to do and when to do them.

As you have surely discovered by now, it is extraordinarily difficult to attend to your bride and her needs instead of getting hypnotized by the constant monologue inside your own head that struggles to understand the mixed signals her behavior may communicate. But, fortunately, you're going to do more than just observe and wait for a to-do list. You have learned the art of bridal communication. So no matter how intensive or relaxed your role as a proactive groom evolves into, you will know that your actions reflect exactly those that your bride wants and needs you to take.

When all is said and done, be sure to thank your bride for your expert groom status. Without her you would have never possessed the desire or had the opportunity to become the savvy groom that you are today. Whether she bought this book for you or you picked it up on your own is irrelevant. What counts is that you made it through the course and came out the other end a wiser groom.

As you embark upon your new life as a new man, never forget your humble roots and how ill equipped you were to help see your bride through the tumultuous travails of wedding planning. You now know never to assume that your bride doesn't need you to be the proactive helpmate you have become. There will always be opportunities to capitalize on your impressive credentials. Make the most of what you know and, as important, always look for opportunities to share your knowledge with other grooms who resemble the sad sack of a groom that you once were.

ABOUT THE AUTHOR

⟨∞⟩

Michael Essany is a published author and columnist who has been
featured on *The Oprah Winfrey Show*
and *The Tonight Show* and in *Time,
People, TV Guide,* and *Entertainment
Weekly* magazines. Michael graduat-
ed with high honors from Valparaiso
University in 2005 with a bachelors
degree in political science.

Photo: Ryan Musch of FH Photographic

Since 1997, Michael has written for and produced local and
national television programs. He hosted the *Michael Essany
Show* for two successful seasons on E! Entertainment Television prior to the program's syndication overseas. He currently
lives with his wife, Christa, in Valparaiso, Indiana, and serves
as the vice president of Indiana Grain Company, L.L.C.

Michael can be reached at MichaelEssany@comcast.net